LOOKING THROUGH TAIWAN

T0340649

**Critical Studies in the
History of Anthropology**

SERIES EDITORS

Regna Darnell
Stephen O. Murray

# LOOKING THROUGH TAIWAN

AMERICAN ANTHROPOLOGISTS' COLLUSION

WITH ETHNIC DOMINATION

KEELUNG HONG

&

STEPHEN O. MURRAY

University of Nebraska Press   Lincoln

Source acknowledgments for previously
published material appear on page 111.

♾

Library of Congress
Cataloging-in-Publication Data
Hong, Keelung, 1943–
Looking through Taiwan: American anthropologists' collusion with ethnic
domination / Keelung Hong and
Stephen O. Murray.
p.   cm.—(Critical studies in the history
of anthropology)
Includes bibliographical references and
index.
ISBN-13: 978-0-8032-2435-3 (cloth: alk.
paper)
ISBN-10: 0-8032-2435-4 (cloth: alk. paper)
ISBN-13: 978-0-8032-2073-7 (paper: alk.
paper)
1. Ethnology—Taiwan—History.
2. Ethnology—Taiwan—Field work.
3. Ethnologists—United States—Attitudes.
4. Ethnologists—Taiwan—Attitudes.
5. Taiwan—Foreign public opinion.
6. Taiwan—Foreign relations—United
States.
7. United States—Foreign relations—Taiwan.
I. Murray, Stephen O.  II. Title.  III.
Series.
GN635.T28H66   2005
306—dc22      2005006497

# CONTENTS

# TABLES

# Series Editors' Introduction

The triumphs of the People's Liberation ("Red") Army in the Chinese Civil War lopped off the buds of social science research on China, both the fieldwork of local researchers and that of foreign ones. The defeated Kuomintang (KMT) and American field Sinologists both retreated across the Taiwan straits. Barred from China, the two groups had a shared interest in (re)presenting Taiwan as "traditional China." The Republic of China (ROC) government—ferried to Taiwan by the American military after the Allied defeat of Japan in World War II—provided ready access to research sites where cooperation with American fieldworkers was close to being compulsory, just as in fieldwork settings for British and French anthropologists in colonial Africa. Both the Chinese oligarchy (the KMT) and the American Sinologists on Taiwan minimized the influence of Japanese education and modernization on Taiwanese during a half-century of Japanese rule and of the earlier influences of European colonial bases on the island, while ignoring the non-Han (Austronesian) substratum of Taiwanese history and culture.

Anthropologists working on Taiwan also ignored the reign of terror and the four decades of an ethnic oligarchy ruling by martial law. The anthropologists wrote about topics such as family structures, healing practices, and religious beliefs, mostly framed as describing pieces of the timeless entity "traditional Chinese culture." As Keelung Hong and Stephen Murray put it, anthropologists were invited by a regime claiming to be the legitimate ruler of China "as if Taiwan was an embalmed Ming-Dynasty theme park for aliens to visit and make their careers writing about as 'Chinese.'" Hong and Murray argue in detail that anthropologists were complicit with the domination of the Taiwanese majority by a refugee Chinese minority and de facto colluded in occlusions of ethnic domination.

Neither the oligarchy nor the anthropologists wanted the persecuted majority to proclaim identity as "Taiwanese" or to consider that there was anything other than Chinese culture on the island field site (for the anthropologists) and that officially it was the base from which to conquer China (for the KMT oligarchy). The formations of consciousness of (being part of a) "kind" that Benedict Anderson wrote about in *Imagined Communities* (1992) depended heavily on media in the local vernacular language. On Taiwan at the time American anthropologists were engaged in field research, any use of the mother tongue of the majority was punished in schools, the majority's language was almost entirely blocked from the airwaves in Taiwan, and it was also mostly absent from the pages of American anthropological publications reporting fieldwork done on Taiwan. Keelung Hong recalls being punished for speaking Holo as a schoolchild and thirsting for broadcasts in the majority language as well as being frustrated by anthropologists who helped to keep the very possibility of conceiving of self and fellows as Taiwanese illicit.

The often biting criticism from Hong and Murray does not keep them from showing that there was some diversity within the American anthropologists' claim to the prestige of working on Chinese rather than Taiwanese phenomena. Products of some graduate schools (especially Berkeley and Columbia) were more likely to represent their work as being about Chinese culture and society than others. Those studying women's labor and entrepreneurship of men or of women mostly did not seek to claim they were studying Chinese culture, while those writing about religion mostly ignored the extent to which popular/folk religion was covert protest against Chinese rule and wrote about essentialized, timeless "Chinese religion."

Although a strength of this volume is its "insider"/"native" perspective, the authors go out of their way to illustrate that insider assumptions are sometimes wrong. Looking at what goes on is important for insider analysis as well as for that of nonnative analysts. The book combines insider and outsider perspectives and provides an extensive discussion in chapter 8 of respectful and disrespectful anthropological perspectives on religious beliefs.

The authors' initial criticisms of American anthropologists' complicity with an ethnic minority's domination were published while the KMT was still in power (during the four-decade "state of emergency"). As American fieldworkers have become welcome in China, most have ceased to work on Taiwan, seeming not to be interested in rapid democratization and the florescence of Taiwanese civil society. The history of American anthropological fieldwork on Taiwan almost entirely ceased when it became possible to undertake fieldwork in China. The post-Mao People's Republic of China remains a Leninist oligarchic regime, like the one that fostered American anthropologists' research on Taiwan from the mid-1950s through the mid-1980s, and remains able to impose foreign researchers in a way that a democratically elected government on Taiwan cannot and does not wish to do. The modus operandi of anthropologists and oligarchs that Hong and Murray criticize has not been forsaken, they argue, only moved to the bigger stage of China that some believed they were looking at while working on Taiwan.

Stephen O. Murray and Regna Darnell

LOOKING THROUGH TAIWAN

# PART I

Introductory Material

# CHAPTER 1

# Experiences of Being a "Native" Observing Anthropology

**B**orn in what was then the Japanese-controlled colony of Taiwan, as were my parents, I (Keelung Hong) grew up in a Chinese colony under martial law. Like Native Americans in reservation schools, my schoolmates were turned into spies to make sure that no one used our mother tongue (Holo/Hokkien). The Chinese imposed names on us in their language, Beijinghua ("Mandarin"), just as they renamed our cities and villages and punished us if we used our native language—even to say one another's names. Like Algerians and Vietnamese reading about "our ancestors the Gauls," we were taught next to nothing about our native land, even its geography (since Taiwanese place-names were being suppressed; instead, we had to learn about locations in China). Our teachers scoffed at the possibility of a Taiwanese culture that was anything other than an inferior copy of Chinese civilization and of any history other than a slow and inept rise from barbarism to second-rate Chineseness. The Chinese whom the U.S. military had transported to Taiwan and left in charge considered Taiwanese barely civilized descendants of pirates and head-hunters. They considered our language corrupted by reduplication-rich Polynesian "baby talk" and punished us for speaking it even in the vicinity of school. In the view of the Chinese who ruled us and tried to suppress our festivals, folk religion, and folk healing, Taiwanese are addicted to "backward, chaotic, and wasteful superstitions" instead of being dutiful followers of the wise and virtuous leadership of Chiang Kai-Shek (Jiang Jieshi).

Although my father was not among the 30,000 Taiwanese slaughtered in the "White Terror" that began in March 1947 and continued into the 1960s, he was forced out of his job so that a Mainlander (*guasienlang*) could take it. Despite the disadvantage of competing in my third language (Beijinghua, the language imposed by the Kuomintang, in contrast to the Holo/Hokkien and Japanese spoken by my family) and systematic discrimination on behalf of Mainlanders against Taiwanese, I did well enough in school to be able to leave and to study in the United States after completing mandatory military service. Emigration was the escape valve for the oppressive system of the Chinese oligarchy, one of the few ways in which Taiwanese of my generation could better our lot. Mainlanders and their children occupied most of the elite positions in the government and the institutions controlled by the government—especially those within universities and research institutes.

When television came along, under the control and close supervision of the KMT state, the government severely restricted shows that were not broadcast in the language of Beijing. Those speaking the majority language (Holo) were portrayed as criminals or menials, reinforcing the Chinese conquerors' views of Taiwanese as inferior, vicious, and too stupid (to speak properly [see Dreyer 2003:5]). Neither our language nor our culture was regarded as "Chinese" by the Chinese, who denigrated us and discriminated against us.

As a graduate student in chemistry first at the University of Texas, El Paso, and later at the University of California, Berkeley, I began reading about the pre-Chinese history of Taiwan and explored American eyewitness accounts of the 1947 reign of terror that silenced political discussion on Taiwan for more than a generation. Although I had an occasional pleasure of recognizing familiar facets of Taiwanese culture, and though I learned many things about Taiwan from reading what has been written in English, I had some unpleasant surprises too. When I began to look at ethnographies of Taiwanese villages, the greatest shock was to see that the customs and beliefs that the Chinese viewed with such contempt and actively sought to eradicate were presented by American ethnographers unable to get into China as aspects of "traditional Chinese culture." Seeing what are supposedly native terms not written in Holo, the language of the people who use these terms, but transliterated into Beijinghua, the language of the people who dismiss our religion and customs, also startled me. Many of the romanizations puzzled me. Without indications of tone, others were ambiguous. Sometimes I was not even certain which language was being romanized!

I soon realized that hardly any of the anthropologists working on Taiwan were interested in Taiwanese culture.[1] While they seemed to be looking at us, they were really looking *through* us to try to see traditional Chinese culture. Most showed no interest in any other part of our historical experiences or with what we made of it (that is, Taiwanese culture). Being invisible or transparent constituted only a slight promotion in the valuation of our culture, because this research done by aliens legitimated substituting the rulers' language for ours and justified subordinating our culture to the so-called great tradition of Chinese civilization. Anthropologists were thereby complicit with the authoritarian ethnic minority oligarchy, to which we were economically and politically subordinate, ruling Taiwan under the fiction of being the "Republic of China," and bemoaned having to be on Taiwan while they dreamed of China. Under martial law during the four-decade "state of emergency," the state-supported "high culture" consisted of heavily romanticized fantasies of life in China. Even Thomas Gold (1994:60), one of the KMT's most loyal and admiring American scholars while it was in power, recalled that "the few works by Taiwanese written in Japanese during the occupation were neglected." It was obvious to me that publications of fieldwork done on Taiwan obliterated recognition of anything Taiwanese in order to claim the more prestigious object of study, Chinese culture. This helped to maintain the Republic of China pretense and keep any "Republic of Taiwan" unthinkable. Similarly, foreign scholars' use of the language of domination was ideologically useful to the KMT in legitimating suppression of the majority's language. The dovetailing of KMT interests and funding (directly by the KMT and the Chiang Chingkuo Foundation and indirectly by Cold War institutions such as the Hoover Institution, the Luce Foundation, and the U.S. government) for research on traditional China on Taiwan was obvious to me. However, I did not know how to enter anthropological discourse to deplore such collusion.

To try to explain my views in English, I enlisted the help of Stephen Murray. Familiar with what anthropologists were writing about anthropologists' eagerness to serve past colonialisms, he helped me to phrase my critique of complicity with Chinese domination of Taiwan in ways that were publishable in anthropology journals.[2] He also was able to suggest some historical reasons why (mostly American) anthropologists stretched their necks like giraffes trying to look across the Taiwan Straits at China while ignoring the fact that they were standing on an island that was becoming "developed" and polluted.

Irritated by an earlier version of the seventh chapter of this book, Hill Gates told me that "anthropologists are not the enemy." While I agree with her that some so-called political science studies touching on Taiwan have shared more "free China" fantasies than have the village and urban neighborhood studies done by anthropologists, the denial of and tacit complicity with derogation and destruction of our language and culture by anthropologists are especially insidious.[3] I have been lectured by sociologists as well as by anthropologists that I am Chinese and that it is wrong to insist on calling myself "Taiwanese." As recently as the late 1990s, at a

World Affairs Council panel discussion on democratization in Taiwan, the Berkeley sociologist Thomas Gold huffily proclaimed that it was "offensive" for a Taiwanese (me) to say that we could decide for ourselves whether we are Chinese. (White American "experts" always know best.) Moreover, those in other social sciences, including many political scientists and most economists writing about Taiwan, have been able to distinguish (and contrast) Taiwanese arrangements from Chinese ones.

I wish that it were true, as Gates maintained, that American anthropologists had helped or were helping to preserve components of our culture. Unfortunately, they cooperated with official ethnocide and linguicide by an army of occupation foisted on Taiwan by the winning side in World War II and recapitulated the practice of ignoring state violence, including ethnocide, against the people studied (earlier ones being anthropologists' relationships with Native Americans and colonized Africans). Furthermore, as soon as they could get the consent of the set of autocrats ruling mainland China, most of the anthropologists who had done fieldwork on Taiwan (including Gates and both Wolfs) moved to their real interest, China. Their departure as democratization (and Taiwanization even of the KMT) accelerated strikes me as an eagerness to collude with another set of oppressive masters, rulers who believe that their legitimacy is enhanced by foreign research describing what the Chinese masters allow to be researched.

This book critically describes what American anthropologists did before they moved on. It is not intended to be a description or even an outline of what Taiwanese culture is but, rather, an interpretive review of the representations of Taiwanese realities in American social science literature, especially anthropology, during the era of KMT authoritarianism.

The next chapter provides a very summary account of American anthropological research on peasants and elaborates on the historical background of anthropological work on Taiwan. Chapter 3 gives a similarly abbreviated historical overview of questions of sovereignty and effective control of Taiwan. Chapters 4–6 discuss American writings on the period before the first American ethnographers arrived on Taiwan, which was the era of White Terror and the Chinese expropriation of Taiwanese jobs, property, and lives.

Anthropology—the social anthropology of Africa, in particular—has been indicted for serving and depending on colonialism (see Foerstel and Gilliam 1992). As Talal Asad (1973:17) put it, "The colonial power structure made the object of anthropological study accessible and safe— because of it sustained physical proximity between the observing Europeans and the living non-Europeans became a practical possibility." Field ethnographers' concern about access to field sites is understandable, but the complicity of alien anthropologists with the Chinese oligarchy ruling Taiwan under martial law (and beyond the termination of martial law) was extreme. It is difficult to imagine, for instance, anthropologists doing research in South Africa, even during the apartheid regime, and presenting Xhosa or Zulu terms translated into Afrikaans as "native terms." The seventh chapter shows that there was variability in the practice of presenting Taiwanese materials as Chinese. The visibility of Taiwanese was greater in some topic areas than others (research on women in contrast to research on religion) and varied systematically according to the place of training (Michigan universities in contrast to Berkeley and Columbia).

The following two chapters confront some of the failings in research methods and in the ethics of Margery Wolf's claims about spirit mediums in the most cited 1990s anthropological publications based on research done on Taiwan—works that, typically, failed to indicate in their titles that the data were quarried (by Taiwanese labor) from Taiwan. The final chapter discusses work done since Margery Wolf's misrepresentations of spirit mediumship and naming practices in Taiwan. After considering the small amount of American anthropologists' research on Taiwan since the lifting of martial law, some of the ways in which American anthropologists protect their own from scrutiny of their linguistic and conceptual incompetence are addressed in the book's acknowledgments.

### The Horror: "That's 'Political'!"

Writing about research funded by the Luce Foundation and the Chiang Ching-Kuo (Jiang Jingguo) Foundation, two bulwarks of legitimating the view of the Chiang Dynasty as "free China," Charles Stafford (2000:168) asserted that, "given the sensitivities surrounding the political status of Taiwan, it was probably inevitable that anthropologists would get caught in the cross fire." Anglophone anthropologists have come under fire, but it is decidedly not "cross-fire," because they have not been in the middle. Rather, they have been securely fed and sheltered within the Chinese ideological lines and have been granted access and given support for their "Sinological" research by the KMT and its foundations. Stafford concluded that, "if anthropologists were to say that Taiwan is not culturally 'Chinese,' they would undoubtedly be accused of promoting Taiwanese independence" (168). It is noteworthy that this sentence has to be in the conditional, because it is a stance that has not been taken by any Anglophone anthropologist. Nor did this anthropologist, who titled his book on education in

Taiwan *The Roads of **Chinese** Childhood*, contemplate the option of writing about what is observed on Taiwan without taking a position on whether it is essentially Chinese or in important ways not Chinese (that is, it is possible to report what he or other anthropologists saw on Taiwan without labeling this as "Chinese culture" or as "Taiwanese culture").

Because my position has been misunderstood (I believe intentionally), I want it to be clear that arguing that the Chineseness of Taiwanese culture has been exaggerated, and that those who have routinely exaggerated it have been complicit with the domination of the ethnic oligarchy, under the two Chiangs does *not* mean that I believe it necessary to show that there is a totally distinctive Taiwanese culture in order to secure for Taiwan the right of self-determination, defined as universal in the United Nations charter.[4] As Ernest Gellner (1983:7) wrote, "It is their recognition of each other as fellows . . . which turns them into a nation, and not the other shared attributes." And "identity is formed and solidified on the basis of common social experience," as Melissa Brown (2004:2) put it. The common social experience of Taiwanese during the era when American anthropologists were doing fieldwork on Taiwan was our exclusion from the life chances afforded to those identified (and to those self-identifying) as Chinese (that is, those who left China in the 1945–49 period and their progeny) and, in many instances, from life itself (see Edmonson in Corcuff 2002; Wong 2001; F. Wang 2002). As early as 1963, Maurice Meisner noted that "Formosans have shared a common historical experience that was and is different and separate from that of mainland China"(105). This experience included recurrent discrimination against and contempt for Taiwanese from those who fled general rejection and defeat in China.

When American anthropologists were working on Taiwan, they depended upon the ethnic oligarchy KMT. The framing of what they wrote about as *Chinese* fit with the blocking of an imagined Taiwanese community and recognition of Taiwaneseness and attempts by a minority ethnic oligarchy to mask the structures of Chinese discrimination against Taiwanese as well as to persecute what were regarded as Chinese beliefs, practices, and use of languages other than the official "national language" (*guoyü*). (The subsequent passing of the presidency to Taiwanese, the splits of the KMT into Chinese and Taiwanese factions and separate parties, is not relevant to the history of the American anthropology of Taiwan, which was almost entirely done before the lifting of martial law and the "Temporary Provisions Effective during the Period of Communist Rebellion," a period that lasted four decades.)

I think that Taiwanese culture differs in significant ways from "Chinese culture" (whether it is traditional Chinese culture of the vanished imperial dynasties or the culture of the contemporary PRC), but, even if there were no differences, the people born on Taiwan should decide for themselves whether they want to be a part of the PRC, a part of Japan, or an independent nation. The islands to the immediate north of Taiwan (the Ryukyus, the largest and best-known of which is Okinawa) had such an opportunity at the end of their occupation by the victorious World War II Allies, and so should Taiwan. Whatever the particulars of Taiwan's linguistic and cultural history, Taiwanese should have the opportunity for self-determination that was proclaimed as a universal right in the United Nations Charter and in Common Article 1.1 of the International Covenants on Civil and Political Rights and the International Covenant on Economic, Social, and Cultural Rights. Common Article 1.1 of the two covenants states: "All peoples have the right of self-determination. By virtue of that right they freely determine their political status and freely pursue their economic, social, and cultural development."

I am *not* arguing for some primordial Taiwaneseness uninfluenced by European, Japanese, and Chinese occupiers (not to mention contemporary American cultural exports). The hybrid that is Taiwanese culture is rooted in forefathers who took great risks in turning their backs on China—many at the urging of European global entrepreneurs—and in our Polynesian foremothers. Contemporary Taiwan—which is economically far more developed than China and is now almost infinitely more democratic—was heavily influenced by twentieth-century modernization programs first of the Japanese Empire (of which it was a relatively content part), then (without direct rule) of the American one. Both of these were (and to a considerable sense still are) regarded as enemies by the PRC, which vaunts its four or five thousand years of superior Chinese civilization and nurtures a xenophobia that was particularly strong during the Qing and Mao dynasties. The linguistic and cultural differences between Taiwanese and Chinese might have mattered less if the KMT occupation of the former Japanese colony had been different. However, the importance of ethnic and linguistic differences between Taiwanese and Chinese were painfully impressed on us by our Chinese overlords, who killed most of our intellectuals (and many others) and who very systematically denied us the same opportunities afforded to the Chinese newly arrived in our midst. Nevertheless, Taiwan's right to self-determination does not depend upon cultural distinctiveness, any more than the American Revolution depended on distinctiveness from English culture.[5]

The systematic representation of the non-Chinese history of Taiwan by anthropologists (and a few sociologists) served to legitimate the ethnic oligarchy that permitted foreign social scientists to work on Taiwan while China was closed to them. Even so ardent an admirer of KMT economic development policies and neo-Confucianism as Thomas B. Gold—at least after the end of the Jiang Dynasty, with the death of Jiang Jingguo (Chiang Ching-Kuo)—forthrightly recognized that the denial of any identity as Taiwanese served to legitimate KMT rule:

> Officially, Taiwan is a province [actually, three provinces] of the Republic of China, with no more claim to a separate identity than any of the other provinces of China [although the others happen not to be ruled by the same government]. Claiming that Taiwan did indeed have an identity different from that of the rest of China which extended beyond the usual dialect [*sic*], cuisine, folkways, etc. opened the Pandora's Box of the island's political future, that is, if Taiwan was not just another Chinese province, then what legitimacy did the Mainlander-KMT regime have to continue to maintain two distinct governments for one island, monopolizing power over the much stronger "central" government. . . . By implication, if it could be shown that Taiwan had a distinct identity, then the island's political structure should be overhauled to reflect this.
>
> Not surprisingly, these questions of identity were raised as part of the strengthening and politicization of civil society. This began to occur as people on Taiwan became aware of their own strength vis-à-vis the increasingly inhibited and vulnerable KMT party-state, of Taiwan's [that is, the ROC's] fragile international existence and of the vast difference between Taiwan's historical experience and that of the rest of China. (1994:59)

Anthropologists who have moved on to the PRC, are beholden to another authoritarian regime, one that claims Taiwan has no important cultural/historical difference from China and an interest in suppressing consideration of such differences (or allowing conquered peoples, notably Tibetans, the right of self-determination). Moreover, these professors' status as Sinologists is higher both in China and in the United States than that of Taiwanologists. There are careerist inducements to support the shared Kuomintang and Chinese Communist Party line that Taiwanese are simply "Chinese." Their imposition of *Chinese* on what they saw in Taiwan is not just indirectly "political." Because it seemed to naturalize Chinese rule and occluded that doing so is political (see Riggins 1997), I would argue that the imposition of *Chinese* on Taiwanese culture is actually **more** political than any recognition of an autonomous "Taiwanese" culture. Elsewhere in the world, anthropologists write about the local. Anthropologists studying Kurdish villages would not translate Kurdish terms into Turkish or Arabic because the Kurdish lands (and entry to them by foreigners) are parts of Turkey, Syria, and Iraq. Anthropologists writing about Catalonia do not substitute Spanish terms for Catalán ones, though Catalonia is a part of Spain and Catalán was officially misrepresented as a "dialect" of Spanish during the Franco dictatorship that was contemporaneous with the Chiang one (see DiGiacomo 2002; Woolard 1988). While anthropologists working in many parts of the world have passed over in silence ethnocide and violence against the people whose culture they write about, citing what people say in the language they use is standard anthropological operating procedure *except* in research on Taiwan.

## Mechanics of the Book

Although presented in the first-person singular, both authors engaged in participant observation in Taiwan beginning in 1943 (Hong) and 1992 (Murray) and participant observation of American anthropology since 1974 (Murray) and 1981 (Hong). The ideas about Taiwanese culture are mostly the first author's, and their formulation in English mostly the second author.

### Romanization of Terms

Despite a tendency to work close to Taipei, where Mainlanders are concentrated, ethnographers have for the most part not studied native speakers of Beijinghua (or other central or northern Chinese languages). Instead, they have studied native speakers of Hakka and Holo (Hokkien, Hoklo, Fujianhua, and Xiamen are other labels for the same language). In common with general anthropological practice everywhere but Taiwan, I endeavor either to render concepts in English or to use native terms, not to translate what is presented as "native terms" into a third language.

Both Holo and Hakka are spoken outside Taiwan—and beyond Taiwan and China, especially by many persons of Han descent in Southeast Asia. Certainly, there are more native speakers of Holo in either China or Taiwan than there are native speakers of all the American Indian languages combined in the United States. Nevertheless, Native American terms from languages with only a handful of speakers are presented in anthropology journals without being translated, for example, into Navajo, the language known to more speakers (and probably to more anthropologists). Not that representation in the fieldworkers' language is neutral either—see Asad

1986:156–60 on anthropologists' textual constructs removed from the scrutiny of those whom these constructs supposedly "represent." But for Holo or Hakka categories obvious translation into English is less insidious than translation into Beijinghua.

A widely diffused myth is that Chinese languages are entirely monosyllabic (that Chinese is the ultimate analytic language). This seems particularly inapt for place-names (toponyms). My renderings agglutinate the syllables without hyphens. I have resisted a strong temptation to do the same thing to personal names (except for my own) but have capitalized the "second word" of personal names because the convention for names in English is to capitalize every separate component, and I would not want to provide any occasion for someone to claim lesser dignity is given to persons with Chinese and Taiwanese names than those with names in European language.

Nicholas Bodman laid out the most widely used romanization of Holo in 1955. Along with the Presbyterian scheme, it uses consonants that are not the ones I hear. I hear *d* where others have written *t, b* where others have written *p,* and *g* for *k* (for example, *dang-gi* for what American anthropologists have written as *tang-ki*), plus *ch* for the *j* sound. What is pronounced *Daiba* is generally rendered *Taipei* in English, and the conventional (mis)spelling appears here in many direct quotations of Anglophone texts. (The acronym KMT is so well established on the basis of *Kuomintang* that the Chinese party is referred to with this old romanization rather than with *Guomindang*.) Buoyed by Bernard (1992), I have rendered the consonants as I hear them. Without extraordinarily technically involved representations, the elaborate tonal aspects of Holo cannot be displayed, so I have not tried to render the complicated (and phonemic) tone differences or to indicate the many glottal stops after the initial consonant (some writers indicate glottal stops for every dental consonant), only those between vowels. The romanizations do not provide sufficient uniqueness for linguistic analysis, but I am not attempting to provide a linguistic analysis of Holo, only to provide some approximation of pronunciation of the terms for persons who cannot speak it.

# CHAPTER 2

# A Brief Overview of American Anthropologists' Investigation of "Others" before 1955

Early American anthropology was nearly entirely focused on Native American (First Nations) peoples (tribes), as their lands were expropriated and their numbers were more than decimated. There was a widespread expectation that such inconvenient reminders of broken promises and wholesale slaughter as Native Americans would disappear altogether. Late-nineteenth- and early-twentieth-century American anthropology was primarily occupied with salvaging memories of pre-reservation aboriginal life and inventorying human cultural traits.

As Bieder (1986), Joyce (2001), and Barnhart (2005) have detailed, even before all the Native Americans had been rounded up and placed in concentration camps (reservations), there was some support in the expansive, relatively new republic of the United States for investigation of "inferior" (that is, nonwhite and/or non-Protestant) peoples beyond the edges of the North American continent. The Wilkes Expedition of 1838–42 was the most important enterprise in expanding American cultural horizons to include Polynesia and South America. Their inhabitants were seen as new "inferior races" to add to the African-American slaves and Native American "barbarians" whom Americans of the Jacksonian era believed they already understood and were predestined to dominate.

The Protestant notion of "God's chosen people" in the "new Zion" of the United States dovetailed with "scientific" notions of "race" and the fitness of American dominion over the continent and beyond. Going out and observing the inferiority of other peoples both justified and prepared for the imperial mission of guiding other peoples up from barbarism to the light of Christian-American civilization—and of determining which peoples could not make the climb to the light and which ones were destined (by God's will, which has often been regarded as coterminous with the self-interest of American domination) to perish.

In contrast to British social anthropologists in Africa, who studied more or less traditional cultures within a system of indirect rule that attempted to preserve local mores and forms of social control, American cultural anthropologists during the late-nineteenth and early-twentieth centuries gathered data of little use to those administering the reservations in which dependents of the U.S. government were maintained in dwindling numbers. Classifying indigenous languages (see Darnell 1971a, b, 1998), had some role in sorting out which wards should go to which holding cell, but preserving (and manipulating) traditional authorities and mores was neither a goal nor a tactic of the U.S. Bureau of Indian Affairs (BIA).

Interest in the lifeways of the vanishing Native Americans was more antiquarian curiosity collection than knowledge to be applied in domination. American anthropologists before the First World War almost entirely ignored the functionings of the reservations and the adjustments of Native Americans to dependency on capricious masters. Eliciting memories of old ways and of languages was not supplemented by research on present-day administration until the New Deal of the 1930s (see Kelly 1985). This new applied anthropology was regarded with considerable skepticism by academic anthropologists such as Alfred Louis Kroeber, but students with no prospects of academic jobs during the Great Depression, including prominent students of Kroeber, began to study the contemporary culture and administration of Native Americans—and, during World War II, of the concentration camps set up for West Coast Japanese Americans (see P. Suzuki 1981; Starn 1986; Ichioka 1989; Murray 1991).

Although depending on the United States government's domination of Native Americans more than aiding in planning, implementing, or evaluating BIA rule prior to the 1930s, American anthropologists had followed American colonialism across the Pacific: to a relatively limited extent in the annexed Hawaiian islands, more so in the Philippine archipelago that had been a Spanish colony before being seized by the United States. Two of the students of Franz Boas who headed major research and training centers, Alfred Kroeber (Berkeley) and Fay Cooper Cole (Chicago), were among the anthropologists who did research on peoples of the Philippines as the U.S. Army put down "rebels" seeking independence and resisting being transferred from one set of colonial masters to another. During and after the Second World War American anthropologists were active in planning for the administration of territories held by the Japanese and German empires and warring against them and the Soviet Empire after World War II (see Foerstel and Gilliam 1992; Price 1998, 2002a, b; Young 2005).

Fieldwork on Taiwan by Japanese anthropologists also focused on aboriginal (Austronesian) "tribes," some of which were pacified and confined to reserves after the last Native Americans were and while some Filipino guerrillas were opposing U.S. occupation of the Philippines. For the Japanese, as for British and American anthropologists, the object of study was the sociocultural organization of "primitives," not peasants or city dwellers. Passin (1947) provided an overview of Japanese research on the aboriginal "natives" of Taiwan.

Lurching back to the mid-1920s: as the supply of "informants" who remembered preconquest Native North American life was running out, American anthropologists' focus on the distribution of aboriginal cultural traits faded. They gradually withdrew from salvaging memories of pre-reservation life from aging Native Americans (see Darnell 1977, 2001; Cole 2003). Anthropologists, particularly in the Midwest, began to pay attention to functioning contemporary cultures, albeit often continuing to look at atomistic traits ("survivals" of aboriginal culture) within a framework of "acculturation" (Redfield, Linton, and Herskovits 1936) and along geographic distributions that continued to be taken as surrogates for historical changes (as in Redfield 1940). Although Native North America fieldwork remained the most common ones for American anthropologists (longer than many have supposed; see Murray 1999), American anthropological fieldwork outside the boundaries of the United States became more frequent after World War I than had been the case before it.

Simultaneously, some anthropologists began to study peoples integrated into nation-state systems (rather than "primitives" and survivors from cultures that were classified as "primitive" who had been segregated on reservations). One concern ("problematic" both in the sense of posing questions for research and difficulties for social control) was with immigrants to American cities (Chicago, in particular) from peasant backgrounds. The "Chicago school" (based in the University of Chicago's sociology department, in which Boasian anthropologists were a cluster of junior partners) focused on urban "disorganization" (anomie, vice, crime) of immigrants to Chicago from rural backgrounds and the uneven assimilation of émigrés from peasant societies outside the United States. The exemplar of research on immigrant peasants in their society of origin and struggling in the United States was *The Polish Peasant in America and Europe* (Thomas and Znaniecki 1918–20). After Thomas was forced out of the University of Chicago, his own more general book, *Old World Traits Transplanted*, appeared under the byline Robert E. Park and Herbert A. Miller in 1921. Park's son-in-law, Robert Redfield, did fieldwork as a graduate student on Mexicans in Chicago and then in Mexico, while his contemporary as a University of

Chicago graduate student, Charlotte Gower, moved from studying Sicilians in Chicago to studying Sicilians in Sicily.

As Murray (2005) details, Redfield and his students, whose ethnographies were published by the University of Chicago Press, established peasantries as within the purview of anthropological discourse and fieldwork. A second clump of anthropologists undertaking fieldwork on peasantries (initially also concentrating on Mexican communities) were alumni of the University of California, Berkeley, anthropology department. Its longtime head, Alfred Kroeber (1948:284), laid out the standard anthropological conception of "peasants" as forming a "part society" ("definitely rural—yet liv[ing] in relation to market towns. They lack the isolation, the political autonomy, and the self-sufficiency of tribal populations"). Neither Kroeber nor his distinguished Berkeley colleague Robert Lowie did research on peasant groups, and, according to George Foster (13 April 2000 interview by Stephen Murray), neither of them ever discussed peasantries in their geographically wide-ranging courses.

Community studies, which previously had been a sociology research specialty, became more common in American anthropology during the 1940s. Redfield had coordinated and theorized (along a folk-urban continuum) social organizations in Mexican villages, and, when Kroeber's most prominent student, Julian Steward (PhD 1929), turned from "primitive" North and South American societies to coordinating a study of Puerto Rico during the late 1940s (work reported in Steward 1956), he also compared villages, chosen for differing economic pursuits rather than along a rural/urban continuum, as in Redfield's Yucatán work. By the time the first American anthropologists set off to do fieldwork in Taiwan during the mid-1950s, agrarian community studies were a legitimate and even prestigious anthropological specialty. As a former student of Robert Redfield more recently argued in specific reference to Steward's comparative work (but of wider applicability, not least to the later Redfield-organized work on "little communities" within literate traditions), "the fact that the separate communities were really parts of a larger whole—the functionally interdependent political economy of the island-nation—somehow escaped the Steward research program and vitiated many of its conclusion. There was no theory of larger systems" (Bennett 1998:87; also see Goldschmidt 1997:viii). This assessment also applies to the village studies done on Taiwan. The Taiwanese villages were represented as exemplars of "traditional Chinese culture" with little consideration of the particular (ROC) state that was exploiting small-scale Taiwanese rice farmers and driving many into decentralized small-scale industrial enterprises.

The disregard for larger (state and economic) systems and tendency to treat communities as isolates—a standard operating practice that had been carried over from the collection of traits of distinct primitive tribes (despite the Boasian focus on geographic and intercultural diffusion of traits)—also characterized the studies of rural Chinese communities that were done in English and American anthropology programs (and influenced by visits by Radcliffe-Brown, Park, and Redfield to the Yanjing University) by native Chinese ethnographers such as Fei Xiaotong, Francis Hsu, Lin Yaohua, Wu Wenzao, and Martin Yang—whether they were analyzing Chinese communities from memory (as in the "native anthropology" exemplar from Malinowski's protégé, Jomo Kenyatta) or from undertaking field research in China (see Guldin 1994:40–48, 62–66).

By the time American anthropologists began to do community studies on Taiwan, large-scale government and foundation funding for area studies had developed in the United States (see Steward 1950; Goldschmidt 1985:167). The communist peasant revolution in China alarmed many Americans,[1] and the American occupation of Japan (which lasted nearly eight years) had broken up rural landholdings there. A market (that is, funding and access to publication) for peasant community studies developed in the United States after World War I (and even more so after World War II), and gauging peasant dissatisfactions that might be mobilized by communists was a concern of those making U.S. foreign policies, though direct Central Intelligence Agency funding of counterinsurgency social science research (in Latin America and Southeast Asia) did not begin until the mid-1960s. Analyzing projected sites of battles and of later military occupation preoccupied many American anthropologists during World War II, and knowledge about other cultures was of strategic interest during the Cold War as well, notably in the interdisciplinary Harvard University Russian Research Center that included anthropologist Clyde Kluckhohn (see Inkeles and Bauer 1961; Price 1998; Robin 2001). Collating information, such as the Human Relations Area Files underwritten by the U.S. Navy, and "culture at a distance" behavioral science analysis of enemies were accompanied by the generation of more data about everyday life and assumptions in what was conceived as a worldwide battleground for the hearts and minds of peasants between godless communism and America(nism) with God on its side, after 1945.

Although those such as Yale University's anthropologist entrepreneur George Peter Murdock, with his U.S. Navy funding and FBI informing on professional colleagues (on which, see Price 2004), were clearly aware of the connections of the research they did or coordinated to the Cold War military and diplomatic establishment, other anthropologists grateful for funding from American foundations (the Ford Foundation was particularly active in funding area research, including Bernard Gallin's pioneering study of a Taiwanese peasant village) and indirect CIA funding followed the admonition not to look a gift horse in the mouth. That is, they did not have to sign directly on to Cold War intelligence gathering or consider what use their descriptions and analyses of alien cultures might be put. Information about cultures, attitudes, and practices of nearly every human group was of potential strategic interest, even in the heyday of loyalty oaths and purging of academic institutions during the late 1940s and early 1950s (see Peace 2004; Price 2004a, b). The surviving base of the anticommunist Chinese (ROC) was of particular concern after the onset of the Korean War and the decision to protect the ROC on its island refuge. The U.S. government did not want peasant rebellions overthrowing regimes allied to the United States anywhere—and especially not in what the leaders of the "free world" called "Free China." Information on the ground gathered by those not obviously spies was welcome by both U.S. and ROC governments. The framing of data gathered on Taiwan as "Chinese" not only provided support for the notion of Taiwan as "Free China" but also was surely read by some (anthropologists and nonanthropologists) as providing insight into those unavailable for scrutiny in China.

# CHAPTER 3

# A Brief Overview of the History of Governing Taiwan

It is uncertain when southern Chinese pirates were joined by peasants from Fujian on the western plain of a large and mountainous island of Taiwan that was divided among chieftaincies speaking mutually unintelligible Austronesian languages. Leaving China was strictly forbidden by successive Chinese dynasties into the nineteenth century. It was Dutch colonists who sponsored the first large-scale migration from southern China to Taiwan in the early seventeenth century. Contrary to the KMT myth (given American currency by anthropologist Stevan Harrell) that Taiwan was settled by Ming loyalists after the Ming Dynasty fell, early settlers violated the Ming ban on overseas travel—cutting themselves off from the most distinctive feature of "Chinese culture," the lineage organizations on the mainland—and intermarried with the aboriginal (Austronesian) population already on Taiwan (Su 1986:13). Clearing land and raising sugar for the Dutch East India Company, the Hokkien-speaking immigrants were involved in agriculture for international markets even before the Ming Dynasty fell in China (Kerr 1986:13–17; Su 1986:11–14; DeGlopper 1995:67).

Prefiguring the KMT in settling on Taiwan after being defeated in China, an army of ostensible Ming loyalists led by a half-Japanese general known in the west as "Koxinga" (Zheng Cheng-Gong) fled to Taiwan and expropriated functioning capitalist agriculture, evicting the Dutch in 1662 (as the KMT took over Japanese enterprises in 1945). After a few decades of what might be called the "Cheng/Koxinga dynasty" on Taiwan, the Qing (Manchu) dynasty in power in Beijing defeated the rebels in 1683–84. However, neither the Ming nor Qing rulers were ever able to control the whole island from Beijing. The Qing government "was not eager to develop its new possession. It held the island mostly because it did not want it used by a hostile power, rebels, or the Japanese and Ryukyuan pirates who were then harrying the coasts of south and central China. The imperial government attempted to restrict migration to Taiwan and considered the island to fall into the same category as the 'South Seas,' the term applied to Southeast Asia" that was not claimed to be part of China despite having many residents of Chinese descent (DeGlopper 1995:91–92). Imperial government bans against overseas travel, migration to, and development of new areas of Taiwan were ineffective, and the greatest influx of population from Fujian and Guangdong occurred in the middle of the Qing era.

Rebellions and interethnic conflict on Taiwan were frequent during the Qing era. Lamley (1981:286) suggested that Qing officials fostered interethnic rivalries to minimize rebellions against the representatives of the overseas government.[1] The extent to which anyone governed Taiwan until the Qing transferred its claims to sovereignty to Japan by the Treaty of Shimonoseki in 1895 is debatable, though no one contends that any Chinese dynasty or government controlled the whole island before 1945 (see Davidson 1903; Kerr 1985:17–29; Su 1986:19–35; W. Hsu 1980; Lamley 1981; Meisner 1963; Meskill 1979; Shepherd 1993). Chuang (1987) estimated that, in the last years before giving Taiwan to Japan, Qing forces controlled only one-third of the island's land mass.[2] The Qing officials sent to Taiwan were classified in the "Fifth service" (the posting most remote from Beijing). The Qing officials imposed the three-tiered land system, a Chinese feudal overlay on European capitalist agriculture on Taiwan. Western lowland Taiwan was a frequently rebellious frontier part of Fujian Province until 1888, when the island became a separate province. In 1895 it was ceded to Japan. An independent republic was briefly proclaimed before the Japanese troops arrived and retreated southward from the beginning of June until the decisive military defeat of President/General "Black Flag" Liu in late October (see Davidson 1903; Morris in Corcuff 2002). Over the course of the next seven years the Aboriginal chieftaincies in the mountains were finally pacified, and the whole island was under the control of the Japanese empire for the first time in 1903 (see Ka 1995).

Japanese colonial investment built important parts of the infrastructure on which the supposed economic "miracle" blossomed, in particular investing in "human capital" through education.[3] Prior to World War II, Taiwan was far more developed than mainland China, particularly in terms of roads and railroads, which made production for export possible all around Taiwan. Despite the slaughter of tens of thousands of the more educated Taiwanese in March 1947, mass education is the cornerstone of the infrastructure of postwar economic development (see Barrett and Whyte 1982),

*Introductory Material*

as in all industrializing societies. "Everywhere, industrialization increased the demand for literate and more educated workers to fill occupations that required longer training than traditional apprenticeships," as Form (2002:151) concluded.

Japan did not "retrocede" Taiwan to China or to any Chinese government. The relevant stipulation in the Peace Treaty of San Francisco of 1951 between Japan and the Allies, to whom Japan had unconditionally surrendered in 1945, is 2.b, which reads, "Japan renounces all right, title, and claim to Formosa and the Pescadores."[4]

During the discussions in San Francisco's War Memorial Opera House (earlier the place where the wording of the United Nations charter, with its proclamation of the universal right of self-determination, had been worked out) in September 1951 in preparation of the peace treaty, representatives of two Soviet bloc governments complained of U.S. aggression in Korea and asserted that Taiwan was an "integral part of China" (the Czech representative, Gertrud Sevaninova) and that there was a "legal right of the Chinese people to Manchuria, Formosa, and adjacent islands" (Polish representative Stefan Wierblowski).

The Japanese representative, Prime Minister Shigeru Yoshida, did not comment on these claims. He confined himself to expressing regret "that disunity prevents China from being here." At no time did he suggest that the Japanese occupation of Formosa/Taiwan or of Korea had been wrong or illegal. Neither did U.S. representatives (Secretary of State) Dean Acheson and (future Secretary of State) John Foster Dulles. (The representative from El Salvador, Héctor Raúl Castro, lauded the renunciation of Korea as "eminently just and legitimate for it puts an end to the unjustified occupation which Japan had exercised over the Korean Nation." He did not, however, find any fault with Japan's occupation of Formosa/Taiwan.)

A "People's Republic of China" (PRC) had been proclaimed two years earlier, and the Kuomintang "Republic of China" (ROC) government had fled to Taiwan earlier. Japan could have transferred its claim to sovereignty to either the PRC or the ROC. Whether Japan could have "retroceded" sovereignty is not entirely obvious. It was the Qing dynasty government that transferred its claims to Taiwan to Japan. The last (long-abdicated) Qing emperor, Pu Yi, was alive in 1951 and, if Japan had transferred its claim to Taiwan back to someone in the Qing dynastic line, it would be proper to speak of "retrocession." Even this completely unlikely scenario might not constitute "retrocession to China," however, within the view that the Qing were a "foreign" dynasty ruling China and the coastal lowlands of Taiwan.

By 1951 the government that had transferred to Japan its claim to Taiwan was long gone, and, if the Manchurian Qing dynasty is not regarded as "Chinese," no part of Taiwan had been ruled by a "Chinese government" from China since the mid-seventeenth century. Japan could not return Taiwan to either the ROC or the PRC, since neither had existed in 1895, nor to the long-gone Ming Dynasty. Also, the resistance of Taiwanese to Japanese occupation in 1895, alluded to by the Czech representative to the San Francisco peace conference, was not an attempt to remain under Qing rule but for the island to be independent.

Japan recognized the "independence of Korea" but not the independence of China or of Taiwan. Had Taiwan been considered a part of China, it would have been covered by provision 4.d—"Japan renounces all special rights and interests in China." At the time Japan surrendered, it occupied a large amount of territory that is now governed by the PRC as well as all of the territory that is now governed by the ROC. If Taiwan were simply a part of China, provision 2.b would not have been needed, only provision 4.d concerning China.

"Retrocession" is an unjustifiable label, long promoted by the KMT/ROC government and still used by American scholars such as Thomas Gold (2003) and Stevan Harrell (Harrell and Huang 1994).

The U.S. military transported its nominal "allies," the Republic of China army that had sat out World War II (see Tuchman 1971), to Taiwan in 1945. After being defeated by the Red Army in China, Chiang Kai-Shek and a half-million of his followers retreated to Taiwan, maintaining martial law under a "state of emergency" until 1987 (followed by de jure repression of any political dissent under sedition laws and a legal ban on the formation of other political parties that was lifted in 1989). Particularly during the Korean War, billions of dollars of U.S. foreign aid poured into the KMT dictatorship. Economic endeavors were the only domain open to native Taiwanese, since government jobs (the prize of competition by examinations in "Chinese culture") were monopolized by the heavily armed ethnic minority, and the traditional Chinese (or universally peasant) goal of acquiring land was blocked and local rentiers expropriated by the KMT (see chap. 4).

Following the death of the occupation army generation (including Chiang Kai-Shek) and successful decentralized industrialization, democratization and Taiwanization began to occur. The first Taiwan-born president was elected by the National Assembly in 1992, directly elected by the people of Taiwan in 1996, and passed the office to the candidate of the opposition Democratic Progressive Party who received the most votes in the 2000 and 2004 presidential elections. Taiwan is now more democratic, with a freer press, than the United States. The focus of this book, however, is on the complicity with an ethnic minority oligarchy's imposition of its official language—one that was unintelligible to Taiwanese when they were subordinated to the Chinese.

# PART II

American Social Scientists'
Complicity with Domination

# CHAPTER 4

# A Case Study of Pseudo-Objectivity

*The Hoover Institution Analysis of 1947 Resistance and Repression*

What had been and was being done to Native Americans was mostly invisible in Boasian accounts of particular Native American cultures and even in the work building on functionalist theorists such as Malinowski and Radcliffe-Brown, who were eager to secure a place for anthropologists in colonial regimes. These complicities with alien domination and the dependence of anthropological fieldworkers upon the approval of colonial administrations have been criticized (once the colonial administrations were no longer around to provide support and protection for visiting anthropologists). Anthropologists' complicity with the domination did not, however, end with the independence of what had been European colonies in Africa and South and Southeast Asia but continued in ideological service to a nonwhite colonial domination on Taiwan. This book details some specific instances, beginning with one not committed by anthropologists, one that provides a retrospective apologia for widespread KMT violence against Taiwanese before any Anglophone anthropologists arrived there.

A particularly egregious example of scholars' complicity not just with domination but with large-scale, genocidal violence is offered by Stanford's Hoover Institution's allegedly value-free political science analysis of the "White Terror," which began in March 1947 and continued into the 1960s. The Hoover Institution was, from its establishment, a foundation of anticommunist intellectual mobilization and remains a place for right-wing officials (such as former California governor Pete Wilson and Ronald Reagan's secretary of state, George Schultz) to enjoy cloistered calm and support in semiretirement from public affairs. It has also long housed apologists for the dictatorship of Chiang Kai-Shek as part of the conflation of anticommunism and places of honor in the "Free World"—this one marked as "Free China."

"Given the powerful political passions that still envelop the 1947 tragedy," Lai Tse-Han, Ramon H. Myers, and Wei Wou claimed in the introduction to their book, *A Tragic Beginning*, published by the Stanford University Press in 1991, "a differentiation of moral and factual issues could be a major step forward in the quest for a just historical judgment" (11). Whether the authors convinced themselves that "justice" is anything other than a moral issue or are attempting to confuse readers is not altogether clear, but the book obviously aimed to exculpate the highest Kuomintang officials, Republic of China president Chiang Kai-Shek (Jiang Jieshi) and governor-general Ch'en Yi (Tan Gi) from responsibility for knowing what KMT troops were going to do (indiscriminate killing of unarmed civilians) when they landed on Taiwan and for the subsequent (somewhat more discriminate) searching out and murder of Taiwanese judged as opponents or potential critics of the regime.

The political "science" to which the authors aspired is taxonomy (Confucian "rectifying names") rather than analysis or explanation. They were particularly eager to classify the events of March 1947, closing their introduction with the admonition from Yin Hai-Kuang, "Whatever something is, that is what you say it is (Shih shen-mo, chiu shuo shen-mo)" (12), and writing that "to call the episode an 'incident' is to place a veil over its actual nature" (8).[1]

"Tragedy" is also a veil, one in which they chose to wrap Chiang Kai-Shek and Ch'en Yi rather than their many victims. "Tragedy" is quite an unusual analytical concept in political science (although "tragedy" is also the category used by the communist leaders of the People's Republic of China for the "Great Proletarian Cultural Revolution" to avoid assessing the responsibility to anyone, especially the party still holding power in China). It may be apt, however, for a number of different interpretations of Taiwanese and Chinese history. For many Taiwanese the first tragedy was that the U.S. Navy transported troops of the Republic of China to Taiwan rather than occupying Taiwan with U.S. or multinational Allied troops. The armies of occupations of the islands to the north of Taiwan (the Ryukus—the largest of which is Okinawa—and of Japan) did not loot the conquered territory, did not dismantle the infrastructure that had survived American bombing, and withdrew after a few years, after supervising free elections. Their record stands in marked contrast to the four decades of martial law and subsequent years of paramilitary rule of Taiwan. An earlier tragedy is that, to keep what Lai et al. (apparently without irony) refer to as the "central government" of Chiang Kai-Shek in the war with Japan, U.S. president Franklin Roosevelt and British prime minister Winston Churchill allocated Manchuria and Formosa to be to the Republic of China in the Cairo Declaration of 1 December 1943, although

Taiwan had not been a part of the ROC or even claimed by it before World War II. (Before Japan invaded China, both Sun Yat-Sen and Mao Zedong advocated independence for Formosa.) Following upon Roosevelt's and Churchill's unconcern for Taiwanese self-determination or for applying the four freedoms that Roosevelt had enunciated as basic human rights, the depredations of ROC officials and troops were predictable, particularly with Ch'en Yi as governor, given the record of corruption and repression he built in Fujian. A number of U.S. military and diplomatic observers of the "central government" in Chunking filed reports on the corruption and incompetence that characterized a dependent ally that played no active part in defeating Japan (see Barbara Tuchman's 1971 account in *Stillwell and the American Experience in China*). U.S. officials also observed and reported upon the plunder and misrule of the island. One of them, George Kerr, later wrote a book based on what he had observed, *Formosa Betrayed* (though it was not published until 1965).

Rather than the tragedy being the jettisoning of the principle of self-determination supposedly maintained by the United States, the tragedy conjured by Lai et al. was the failure of Taiwanese to appreciate the frustrations and travails of the army of occupation allocated to them and that, rather than appreciating the systematic looting of the island, Taiwanese were instead dismayed by ROC corruption, incompetence, and brutality. "The tragedy was a reflection of China's struggles in the 1940s to turn itself from a traditional society into a modern one, with an efficient democratic government," according to Lai et al. (11). It is difficult to know what this statement means. Who is the "China" that was struggling and seeking "democracy"? Is a "reflection" an epiphenomenon? Are Taiwanese people and their reactions epiphenomenal, determined solely by events and patterns on mainland China? That Lai et al. wrote of Taiwan as "one small part of China" in the same paragraph (and elsewhere) supports this last interpretation. Such a characterization is anything but neutral, either in the context of 1947 or in that of current PRC claims of sovereignty (and continued U.S. support of a "one China" policy that obliterates Taiwan).

"One small part of China" is a telltale sign that the authors adopted the perspective of the Chinese (Kuomintang and Communists) as the legitimate rulers of Taiwan. From this perspective—and only from this perspective—"whether the dissidents' acts in February and March amounted to sedition is a factual question that lacks a moral dimension" (10), though there are few "crimes" more wrapped in morality in Chinese conceptions than sedition. Even after the lifting of martial law in 1987, the KMT government treated advocacy of independence for Taiwan as sedition.

Whether the only army of occupation from World War II still holding power when Lai et al. wrote should have been able to define *sedition* (or, indeed, to define *law* in general) is a question with a moral dimension that they ignored. There can only be "sedition" against a legitimate government, and the legitimacy of KMT rule of Taiwan is a question Lai et al. carefully avoided raising.

There are many instances of uncritical adoption by Lai et al. of KMT historical perspectives. One of the most egregious is the interpretation of the 1895 declaration of Formosan independence as evidence of Taiwanese "patriotic attachment to China" (44). The "patria" of that patriotism, however, was Formosa, not China. There was a declaration of independence, **not** a declaration of continued loyalty to China or to its alien (Manchurian) regime. It is understandable that the KMT would seek to misrepresent the meaning of the declaration, but, when ostensible "scientists" follow this party line, their allegiance to the KMT is hard to deny.

The authors participated in (rather than analyzed) a number of KMT definitions of a number of past and present situations. "Restoration" or "recovery" by a government (or party) of a territory it had never previously ruled has already been mentioned (and examined closely in the survey of sovereignty in the previous chapter).

Full of sympathy for the difficulties of governing China, the authors bewailed that in the late 1940s, "knowing little about what had happened on the Mainland during Word War II, many Taiwanese never appreciated the seriousness of the problems confronting the Nationalist government in 1945" (50).[2] Lai et al. did not explain why Taiwanese should have been grateful or loyal to a government they had neither elected nor sought. Moreover, it is very dubious that knowing more of the record of corruption and retreat that was the story of the KMT during World War II would have increased enthusiasm for the regime. Lai et al. admitted that, before the Japanese invasion, "China remained afflicted by warlordism, even in the KMT's base area of Chekiang and Kiangsu," and that, on the mainland, "the KMT was never able to expand its membership beyond 600,000, which constituted only about 0.003 percent of the country's total population (52). Aside from the fact that these numbers do not make sense together (requiring there to have been 20 billion Chinese, whereas the 1953 census enumerated 583 million, and the usual KMT estimate for the population on the eve of the Japanese invasion was 450 million), it is difficult to imagine anyone seeking so unpopular a party to provide "tutelage in democracy."

Lai et al. seem to have been unable to conceive that anyone (in the 1940s or the 1990s) could question the KMT right to rule Taiwan as a part of

China. They did not see anything wrong with the KMT view of Taiwan "as primarily a source of resources with which to fight important battles on the Mainland. In fact, Mainlanders (*guasienlang*) felt that, because Taiwan enjoyed greater wealth and higher living standards than the Mainland, Taiwanese should carry a heavier burden than other Chinese in the struggle to defeat the Communists and modernize" (169) and assert that "the KMT worldview was not unreasonable. The KMT was trying to save China from Communism, seeking values in the Confucian tradition of indigenous civilization, and pursuing unification and modernization of China according to Sun Yat-sen's vision" (179).

Although Lai et al. think that it would have been wise for the army of occupation not to alienate the populace, they do not consider the consent of the governed important (or representation as a prerequisite for legitimate taxation, though that was a principle fought for in the American Revolution). They recognized that "people like the P'engs [Peng Ming-Min] saw the KMT as an institution that would drag Taiwan down to the level of Chinese backwardness" (21) but could only conceive the problem with ROC critics of Peng's generation as deriving from a lack of "conceptual access to the evocation of Confucian ideals that was to become central to the ideology and culture of Taiwan under the KMT" on the part of those exposed to (or, in the KMT view, contaminated by) liberal Western and Japanese ideas (22). Such Taiwanese intellectuals were also offensively (in the view of the KMT and of Lai et al.) aware of Chinese isolation and backwardness in contrast to Taiwan's longtime participation in the world economy. "Nothing was more offensive to the Mainlanders than the idea of looking up to the Taiwanese elite as Japanese-trained experts on modernization when Chinese had just fought and defeated the Japanese," Lai et al. claimed (50). Yet, as Chang Chun-Hung (1987) wrote, after the transfer from Japanese to Chinese rulers:

> we [Taiwanese] immediately began to sense the conflict of culture. Moreover, that conflict of culture was extremely intense. It was discovered that the Japanese culture which we had originally loathed was, as compared to the culture of our fatherland, a strong culture, a superior culture. And the culture of the [KMT] rulers is a worthless, inferior—an inferior kind of barbaric culture. (Quoted in Wachman 1994:95)

The relatively greater development of Taiwan in contrast to China in 1945–47 cannot seriously be contested, so Lai et al. de-emphasized it.

Neutral observers would be surprised by the claims that the KMT had "defeated the Japanese," wondering what battles the ROC armies won and how the "central government" happened to be in so peripheral a location as Chungking and, even after Japan surrendered, could not get to Taiwan on its own (62). Taiwanese most certainly had *not* seen ROC troops defeat Japanese troops. No one had! The ROC military continued to demonstrate the same prowess and tactical genius in Manchuria and elsewhere during the late 1940s that it had demonstrated during the war with Japan. To claim that in 1945 the KMT was moving from the stage of "tutelage" to that of "constitutional rule" is almost as peculiar and disingenuous as to cast it as defeating the Japanese Empire (51).

   Governor-General Ch'en Yi refused to speak Japanese, although he appears to have been more fluent in it than he was in Beijinghua, the official language imposed by the KMT, and although practically no Taiwanese understood Beijinghua. (Moreover, those who did had difficulty understanding either Ch'en Yi or Chiang Kai-Shek when they tried to speak it.) Ch'en Yi's government used the fact that "most former Taiwanese officials could not speak *kuo-yü* ('the national language') and were not trained to work in a Chinese administration" to justify replacing those who had "collaborated" with the Japanese "enemy" (to which an earlier Chinese regime had ceded Formosa in 1895) with Ch'en Yi's Mainlander cronies and followers. (The replacement of Taiwanese by Mainlanders in government monopoly businesses continued during the 1950.) Officials, from Ch'en Yi down, did not speak or refused to speak the languages (Holo, Hakka, and Japanese) that Taiwanese understood. This language policy guaranteed that Taiwanese perceived the government as alien. It indicated unmistakably the view of the Taiwanese as a conquered people without rights that underlay the conduct of Ch'en Yi's government of Taiwan. Lai et al. found Ch'en Yi's refusal to use Japanese "understandable," although they recognized that his language policy contributed to the estrangement of Taiwanese that led to their revolt.

   Another of Ch'en Yi's tactical mistakes, in the view of Lai et al., was permitting relative freedom of the press. Apparently, they were shocked (in the mid-1990s) that an article in the *Ho-p'ing jih-pao* published on 8 August 1946 "emphasized how the Taiwanese sincerely wanted democracy, and gave readers the impression that the administration was not sincerely trying to fulfill those hopes." How could anyone have questioned the KMT's sincerity about democracy? They were similarly astounded that "reports often depicted complex events in a way that made the administration seem inept. . . . Given the freedom to criticize the government, the press often did not provide balance" (77). Lai et al. provided plenty of evidence of the ineptness of the administration. Although the authors were imbued with compassion for the sufferings and loss of face of the backward KMT officials, they did not take seriously the frustrations Taiwanese—who were accustomed to efficient and uncorrupted Japanese administration—felt.

Immediately after noting a lack of balance in the press before March 1947, Lai et al. wrote, "After the spring of 1947, when the press became more strictly controlled, it blamed the Uprising on the 'poisonous' influence of Japanese colonial rule, underworld elements, and riffraff" (77–78), leaving this official view as an apparent example of the balance so sadly lacking before March 1947.[3] Probably not coincidentally, their example of balance corresponds to the explanation for the revolt offered by Ch'en Yi:

> Ch'en began by arguing that the Taiwanese had lost their understanding of Chinese culture and their spirit of nationalism because of 51 years of Japanese rule. He then blamed the press for criticizing his administration and for sowing seeds of dissension between Taiwanese and Mainlanders. He blamed the Japanese wartime mobilization programs for the anti-Chinese attitude of many urban young people, especially those who had returned from places overseas, like Hainan Island. He also blamed Taiwanese business people for not recognizing how publicly [that is, KMT] owned enterprises had contributed to the island's recovery. (150–51)

Yet Lai et al. joined the Taiwanese of the 1940s in not recognizing economic recovery attributable to state monopolies. They also recognized at least the corruption and incompetence of the Ch'en Yi's government, although they went to considerable lengths to exculpate him personally. For instance, they asserted that "no one could criticize the Governor-General for corrupt behavior" (78). Even if Ch'en Yi did not enrich himself, he presided over looting by his subordinates and bought support by retaining these subordinates.[4] "He took no action against them, even if they turned out to be corrupt or incompetent," as the authors admit (79). Complicity with corruption is corrupt, and we will falsify Lai et al.'s statement by saying that we criticize Ch'en Yi for corrupt behavior, even if he was as personally frugal as they claim. It was his policy to give control to his subordinates of what had been Japanese private as well as public enterprises. If he did not know what they were doing, he was incompetent. If he did know, he was a partner in corruption, however low a share he took for himself. In any case, more than a "development strategy" of "statism" was involved. Moreover, the record of corruption, including extensive trading with the enemy (then Japan) while Ch'en was governor of Fujian makes Lai et al.'s attempt to distinguish his depredations from the rampant corruption of his misrule of Taiwan implausible.

Besides minimizing Ch'en Yi's responsibility for undermining the economy and social order, Lai et al. waxed lyrical about the hardships of "mainland officials who had arrived on the island with the sincere intention of reuniting the two societies [but] became frustrated and bitter" at the Taiwanese lack of sympathy for the rigors of "public service" they suffered: "Life in a semi-tropical environment required adjustment, and officials, most of whom could not bring their families, experienced loneliness and frustration" (95). Of course, being posted to someplace distant from one's family was an essential feature of traditional Chinese governance (designed to limit enriching the extended families of officials). Moreover, Japanese officials seem to have adjusted to the semitropical environment, although Japan is north of the birthplaces of most of the KMT officials who fled to Taiwan during the 1940s.

Despite having acknowledged the substantial mismanagement of the economy and the rampant corruption and misrule that were undermining the rule of law that had characterized the Japanese era, Lai et al. at no point questioned the legitimacy of KMT rule of Taiwan. They judged Ch'en Yi and many of his officials as "honest" and "sincere" (though not revealing their metric for the unusual political science task of gauging "sincerity"). They see the officials they know to have been extremely corrupt and completely indifferent to the consent of the governed as unjustly maligned by Taiwanese (in the 1940s and since). Ch'en Yi and his government would have been wiser to have proceeded differently in the authors' view, but Taiwanese should have been willing to be expropriated for the struggle against communism on the mainland by some residual Chinese patriotism and some Confucian sense of duty to accommodate armed aliens. Lai et al. seem to consider this another factual, rather than moral, judgment. Although they believe that the population of Taiwan owed the KMT obedience and should have ignored the mismanagement of the economy and society that Taiwanese experienced in 1945–47, they nowhere have explained *why* they believe this. Nor did they identify any point at which they think that revolt against misrule is justified.

Only within the framework of a legitimate government can sedition be a "factual question" (10), and, even then, it is likely to be contested and adjudicated. Lai et al. counterfeited objectivity within a circumscribed realm of legitimacy to argue that, during the first days of March 1947, "demands escalated and that they took on a revolutionary character is indisputable" (99). Again a few pages later, the self-styled objective social

*Complicity with Domination*

scientists note that, because some of the "demands would have in effect ended the sovereign authority of the ROC in Taiwan, they can be called 'revolutionary' " (102). Their own chronology shows that the 32 Demands of the Taipei Resolution Committee made on 7 March (two days **after** Chiang Kai-Shek had dispatched troops to crush the rebellion) were withdrawn on 8 March (before the troops arrived) and belies their conclusion that the first trajectory, increasing radicalization of dissident demands, caused the second trajectory, the central governments' shift from conciliation to repression (177).[5]

Despite taking great pains to plaster the category "revolutionary" onto some Resolution Committee proposals, Lai et al. adamantly refused to characterize what happened as a "revolution." They do not want to veil what happened between 28 February and 8 March 1947 as merely an "incident," but they also do not want to accede that there could have been a Taiwanese revolution. Although not approving of the amount—or, at least, the indiscriminateness—of the terror that followed the arrival of reinforcements for the garrison army, Lai et al. maximized estimates of the Chinese casualties in the first days of March and minimized estimates of the Taiwanese casualties beginning in the early hours of 9 March 1947.

On page 159 Lai et al. considered the judge's mention of "several thousand" casualties, rather than "more than 10,000," in the trial of Monopoly Bureau officials charged with instigating a riot as evidence that the number was less than 10,000. One can think of many reasons for a ROC judge not to mention the number of casualties even had he known their number. Lai et al. did not discuss allegations that some Taiwanese corpses were dressed in army uniforms or the attempts to use the official registries to estimate the number of Taiwanese who were killed in 1947. Provincial councilwoman Chang Wen-Yin contrasted the 1948 death rate with the 1947 data to estimate that 19,146 were killed in the first ten months of the KMT White Terror. To the horror of the official inquiry contracting it, Chen Kuan-Zheng's modeling of fatalities based on disappearances of names from household registries and expected deaths from natural causes raised estimates of fatalities to 100,000 (reported in the *Taiwan Tribune*, 20 January 1992) and included a conservative estimate of between 18,000 and 28,000. When Chiang Ching-Kuo had the police household registries cleaned up, the number of unaccounted-for persons was 123,457 (reported by historian Su Bing in the 25 February 2004 *Taiwan Daily*). Yet anthropologists such as M. Brown (2004:252 n. 10) continue to parrot the discredited low estimates of Lai et al. (1991).

Note the use of the passive in the following: "Killings occurred, trials were conducted, people involved in the recent Uprising were imprisoned and in some cases innocent people were persecuted" (151). [6] The innocent people who were officially persecuted were all Taiwanese. Almost all the killings were done by ROC soldiers and policemen. All the trials were conducted by ROC judges. All the imprisonments were ordered by ROC judges. Just as Lai et al. did not hold Ch'en Yi responsible for the conduct of his government in 1945–47, they exculpated Chiang Kai-Shek and his commanders for the massacres, beginning with the landing of troops in Keelung on 9 March, "spray[ing] the wharves and street with gunfire, shooting anybody on sight" (156).

No more than the corruption of ROC officials on Taiwan could the conduct of ROC troops have been a surprise to Chiang Kai-Shek or to Ch'en Yi, for "the tactic of shooting indiscriminately at people and houses had long been used by KMT troops and warlord armies on the Mainland when putting down opposition" (156). Lai et al. repeated without questioning Ch'en Yi's claim that "he had not anticipated the vindictive behavior of the troops" (178) and wrote that "Chiang Kai-Shek and Ch'en Yi could not have been expected to control those divisions and regimental commanders and officers who rounded up and shot unarmed citizens, secretly disposed of their bodies, and strafed residences and shops" (161).

Considering that Ch'en Yi requested the troops and that Chiang Kai-Shek dispatched them, this is one of the most peculiar statements in the entire book. The governor-general and the president/generalissimo may not have issued specific orders to gun down unarmed civilians upon landing, but both have to have known that this was more than likely and to have expected it. (Finally, in February 2003, Lai acknowledged this.) Someone issued specific orders to seize "revolutionaries" in subsequent days. Lai et al. did not trace the origins of these lists (nor is there any evidence they made any serious effort to do so), however, and guidance of this systematic roundup of purportedly "disloyal" intellectuals cannot be attributed to rowdy troops that had just landed.

Lai et al. wrote, "Our sources are silent about who provided the lists of people for Nationalist troops to arrest, imprison, and even shoot" (164). There is no indication that Lai et al. made serious attempts to find out who ordered that the lists be made. With similar(ly motivated) lack of diligence, they were only able to find one account by a military participant and did not mention asking about it in the "around 60" interviews they conducted. They mentioned being granted permission to examine the records of the Garrison Command in Taipei without ever being able to gain actual access to them (12), but it seems they did not try very hard to find out who

*Complicity with Domination*

supplied lists of Taiwanese to round up or to elicit accounts of officially sanctioned violence.

Chiang Kai-Shek and Ch'en Yi were in command and responsible for what occurred. Neither of them issued orders against the conduct that Lai et al. acknowledge was standard operating procedure for ROC troops—conduct that would constitute war crimes in an international conflict and are arguably the same kinds of genocidal "crimes against humanity" for which former Yugoslavian president Slobodan Milosevic is being tried in the Hague.

Although they are fully aware that Ch'en Yi requested reinforcements and Chiang Kai-Shek decided to send the 21st Division on 5 March 1947, Lai et al. repeated Chiang's disingenuous rationale of 10 March: "Last Friday, March 7, the so-called Feb. 28th Incident Resolution Committee unexpectedly made some irrational demands" (147). Demands made on 7 March were irrelevant to what had been decided two days earlier. Such a public statement provides dubious "pinpointing" of what was significant in Chiang's decision on (or before) 5 March. Taking after-the-fact public pronouncements as adequate analyses of motives is a dangerous methodology for political science, all the more so for ones claiming to assess sincerity. To claim that demonstrably anachronistic accounts pinpoint motivation is to participate in, rather than to analyze, an ideology and shows yet again that Lai et al. are apologists for the KMT rather than the objective scientists they claim to be.

The authors revealed their involvement in KMT ideology of the 1990s (yet again) in their trivialization of advocacy for independence by some Democratic Progressive Party leaders "because they lacked any other significant issue . . . to woo voters from the KMT" (184). Along with their sponsor, Thomas Metzger, Lai et al. remain unwilling to take seriously that any Taiwanese (at any past or present time) seeks independence for Taiwan. Since the end of World War II most places that were colonies before the war have achieved independence. Peoples suppressed for decades by Leninist regimes from the Baltic and the Balkans to the Pacific have struggled to establish independent states. Yet the purportedly objective social scientists who planned and wrote *A Tragic Beginning* were unable to conceive that anyone but gangsters and terrorists would challenge the legitimacy of the Leninist regime foisted on Taiwanese after World War II. To them nationalism, "common in our century," is reasonable if it is Chinese but unreasonable if it is Taiwanese (179). What could be more objective?

If the authors were genuinely concerned with making a contribution to political science rather than with minimizing the culpability of the

KMT/ROC for the massacre of tens of thousands of Taiwanese civilians, one might expect comparison to other revolutions, successful or failed, or at least to comparison to other occurrences of urban revolts in Chinese societies.

*A Tragic Beginning* is **not** a contribution to a comparative science of politics. Although it marks an advance from the absurd traditional KMT "explanation" of communist agitation as the cause of dissatisfaction in Taiwan in 1947 by acknowledging the incompetence and corruption of Ch'en Yi's administration, the book is still an attempt to exculpate Ch'en Yi and Chiang Kai-Shek. Despite claims to being "factual" and "objective" and not making moral judgments, Lai et al.'s underlying assumption that the KMT government (in the early 1990s and the late 1940s) was legitimate and that advocacy of independence is illegitimate is not a factual judgment nor a matter of science. The authors are either incapable of differentiating fact and value or deliberately misrepresented what they were doing in their book, which is based on and filled with antidemocratic values. Whether one judges their neoconservative, neo-Confucian values as moral or as immoral, their pretense of objectivity was fraudulent. Directly and indirectly—as employees of the ROC and of the Hoover Institution, to which the ROC has given considerable sums of money, whether or not any ROC funds were allocated specifically to financing the research and writing of this book—they were paid apologists for the Kuomintang and its fantasy state, the "Republic of China."

# CHAPTER 5

# Some American Witnesses to the KMT's 1947 Reign of Terror on Taiwan

L ike many Taiwanese who grew up puzzled about what happened in 1947 that so traumatized any open political discussion (and especially any open criticism of the KMT), once in the United States, I (Keelung Hong) sought out anything I could find about the brutal response to the so-called 2/28 incident and found that some Americans who were on Taiwan during the late 1940s had written about the reign of terror.

In the summer of 1986 a group that included Yang Chonchung, Stephen Murray, and me went to Grass Valley to talk to one of them. Ed Paine had been a lieutenant in the U.S. Army at the end of World War II and was assigned to the Relief and Rehabilitation Unit of the United Nations. Like George Kerr, author of *Formosa Betrayed*, Ed Paine was frustrated that, instead of reconstructing what had been damaged by U.S. bombing, KMT officials were lining their pockets and shipping off to China anything of value that could be moved (including railroad rolling stock and most of the rice and sugar produced on Taiwan). From direct contact with officials put in charge of Taiwan by the Allies (and transported to Taiwan by the U.S. military), he learned that, before losing the mainland, Chiang's underlings considered Taiwanese as "enemy aliens" to exploit, not "Chinese brothers." Residing in Daiba (Taipei) in March 1947, he was a horrified observer of the bloody arrival of KMT troops.

For Paine, even after more than forty years, the horrible sight of corpses floating in a blood-red Keelung River remained the unforgettable part of KMT reassertion of domination. He had heard gunfire the night Chiang Kai-Shek's troops landed in Keelung but had not realized the scale of indiscriminate slaughter that began then.

In the following weeks he learned of the more carefully planned murders of educated Taiwanese. He reported what he observed to Washington at the time. After returning to the United States, he wrote letters to Congress and various news agencies seeking to raise concern about what he had seen. He showed us various letters, some of which were published, and the noncommittal bureaucratic responses he received.

For a time he and George H. Kerr worked on a book manuscript. Although they had received an advance from a publisher, Kerr stopped work on the book without giving Paine any satisfying explanation and only much later (1965) published *Formosa Betrayed*. That book is very critical of Chiang and his subordinates. It would have had a greater impact, however, closer to the time of the events (and closer to the time when it appears to have been written). Stephen Murray wrote to Kerr asking about the sequence of writing and publication of *Formosa Betrayed*, but in two letters Kerr avoided the direct (and repeated) question of why a book about his observations did not appear much earlier. (My guess is that the virulent attack on American experts for "losing China" in part for reporting the unpopularity of Chiang Kai-Shek had traumatized and/or deterred him, but this is a surmise for which I have no evidence.)

Ed Paine also told us that he had recommended a young Taiwanese with whom he had worked to translate for (Captain) Vern J. Sneider when Sneider came to Daiba. Sneider's first novel, *Teahouse of the August Moon* (1951), is a bemused account of the education of a U.S. Army of Occupation officer by Okinawan villagers. It was a best-seller, the basis for a hit Broadway play, a Hallmark Hall of Fame television production, and a movie (in which Marlon Brando played the Okinawan employee of Glen Ford; it was released on video in 1990).

The book Sneider wrote about Taiwan, *A Pail of Oysters*, published in 1953, also contains some amused accounts of an American's incomprehension of Pacific Islanders' ways of doing things that is similar to the central comedies of intercultural misunderstandings in *Teahouse of the August Moon* and in *The King from Ashtabula* (1960), his later novel about a Micronesian student in Missouri who suddenly is recalled (by another U.S. Army occupation) to be king of an American-administered island.

*A Pail of Oysters* is much less lighthearted than those more popular works of fiction. It describes not just the foibles of confused Americans out of their depths across the Pacific but accounts of KMT terror, including the shooting of the character based on the interpreter Ed Paine recommended to Vern Sneider. The book opens with a KMT patrol seizing oysters gathered by Taiwanese coast dwellers. The first chapter also appeared as a story in a 1950 *Antioch Review* and was reprinted in the 1956 collection of Sneider's short stories, *A Long Way from Home*, most of which were set in Korea. Sneider makes very vivid the terror in which Taiwanese lived during the late 1940s, under the oppression of KMT bandit troops. He also makes clear the common Taiwanese views that what land reform was really about was breaking up any Taiwanese power bases.

Hollywood did not evidence the same interest in *A Pail of Oysters* as in his other books. Although well reviewed, it was not a popular success. Even more than *Formosa Betrayed*, copies of *A Pail of Oysters* disappeared from most libraries, probably on instructions issued to the student spies paid by the KMT to monitor Taiwanese on U.S. college campuses.

Informed estimates of the extent of killings of Taiwanese continue to mount. Despite the attempt of a Hoover Institute book to downplay both the number of fatalities and the responsibility of the "Republic of China" government, since the lifting of martial law, scholars in Taiwan have finally been able to discuss the extent of the horror. *A Pail of Oysters* continues to provide a vivid contemporary picture of the terror in which adult Taiwanese lived in the late 1940s, and a Taiwanese translation by Gou Eng-Chu was published in 2003 by Avant-Garde.

CHAPTER 6

# Studies of KMT-Imposed Land Reform

**E**valuating the impact of land reform was a central problematic of early research by American anthropologists on Taiwan (Bessac 1964, 1967; B. Gallin 1963, 1964, 1966; Koo 1968; Yang 1970). These scholars did not prescribe it as a model, probably realizing that such a policy can only be carried out by an alien regime without local ties. As Amsden (1979:37) noted in analyzing Taiwan as an exceptional case: "Taiwan's land reform was engineered exogenously, by the Kuomintang, in alliance with the Americans. The Taiwanese landed aristocracy could be expropriated because the Americans and Mainlanders were under no obligation to it. This was a most unusual situation, and unlikely to be repeated."

Anthropologists are more reluctant than political scientists to praise military conquest as the royal route to progress, whether or not they understood the impact and extent of the KMT slaughter of Taiwanese in 1947. Moreover, they appear to realize that not just rural landowners but agricultural productivity was sacrificed to promote the industrialization of Taiwan in a series of government policies made without any popular input.

Another obstacle to explaining the process and the outcomes is that there were no anthropologists observing the decision making of the central government nor rural aspirations in the late 1940s and early 1950s nor even the implementation of various land-to-the-tiller laws between 1948 and 1953. Anthropologists arrived in Taiwanese villages only *after* the fact and tried to estimate the effects of land reform on rural social structures retrospectively.

Martin Yang, the author of one of the pioneer community studies from China, *A Chinese Village* (1945), in his 1970 book, *Socio-Economic Results of Land Reform in Taiwan*, reported the results of a 1964 survey by 30 interviewers of 1,250 former tenant farmers, 250 current tenant farmers, 250 former landlords, and 100 nonfarmers from five regions. Those who were still tenant farmers after land reform provided a control group for comparing the direct effects of these policies. Yang found relatively equivalent rates of adopting various "modern" characteristics by tenant farmers and by former tenant farmers, which indicated that land reform was not an important cause of other changes viewed as "modernization." For instance, an 84 percent increase in voting for village head by former tenants was matched by an increase among tenants of 83 percent; a 75 percent increase in consulting Western-style physicians by former tenants was surpassed by a 113 percent increase by tenants, and so on through family roles and acceptance of agricultural innovations. Although the data are not always presented in ways permitting comparison,[1] and although the questions about approval of land reform were quite general and framed by what most people thought rather than what the individual men questioned thought, most former tenants considered land reform positively, and so did Yang. He was, however, concerned that fragmentation of landholdings would make further agricultural development difficult. He warned, "The land problem in Taiwan is far from being resolved. . . . Redistribution of land-ownership might later become a hindrance to the development of a modernized agriculture. . . . The smallness of the farms [after land reform] is such a serious deterrent to modernization and mechanization that significant advances can hardly be hoped for" (258–59).[2]

Bernard Gallin (1963) also noted the small and fragmented holdings of farmers in the village he studied in the late 1950s. He reported that less than half the farmers did not realize any cash from their crops. He also reported (in his table 13) a slight decrease in land cultivated, in contrast to 1949–51, and noted that, when the tax burden was added to the mortgage payments, farmers who had been tenants on public lands (primarily holdings of the Taiwan Sugar Corporation) were paying more of their crops than before the sale of the land (96–97). He concluded that the Land-to-the-Tiller Act

> in itself had not brought any noteworthy increase in the standard of living. . . . Villagers who work outside of Hsin Hsing [the village he studied, Xin Xing in pinyin] have done more to raise the standard of living than has the decrease in tenancy. The increased use of cash has also led to an apparent rise in living standards. In Japanese times, villagers tended to save their money toward future land purchases. Today, people no longer save money for fear of inflation. (108–9)

Gallin also noted that a result of the static land market was "an ossification of socioeconomic mobility within the rural area" (120), pushing aspirations into business and out of agriculture, if not completely out of the countryside.

In contrast to Gallin's and Yang's careful consideration of land reform in the context of various social changes with varying unanticipated effects, Anthony Koo compiled data on increased agricultural productivity and income on Taiwan after 1948. Since he did not disaggregate data by size of landholding, nor by change in ownership, his attribution of all changes in the agricultural sector to land reform was more an act of faith or an instance of the *post hoc ergo proper hoc* fallacy than it was an analysis of differential effects of various changes in agriculture on Taiwan in the 1950s and 1960s. It was hardly the case that everything except land tenure remained constant in rural Taiwan during those decades so that changes could clearly be attributed to land reform. Chen Hsiang-Shui (1977) argued that there was only an indirect relationship between land reform and increased productivity, that trends in the latter preceded land reform, and that they depended on the acceptance of technological changes such as hybrid seeds, fertilizers, and insecticides.

Longer-term trends in agricultural development on Taiwan fit Chen's view better than Koo's. Within the long history of non-subsistence agriculture in Taiwan, Myers and Ching (1964) questioned whether equality in land tenure is a prerequisite of agricultural development, given that

> Taiwan under Japanese colonial rule achieved rapid and sustained agricultural growth despite widespread tenancy and very unequal land distribution. The Japanese successfully repeated the institutional organizational and reforms, tested during the early Meiji period, of working through the landlords and wealthy farmer class to encourage the introduction of innovations into agriculture. (555)

They singled out improved seeds as the most important change leading to increased productivity during the Japanese era. While concurring on the importance of technological improvements, especially successful adaptation to Taiwan of seeds with high yields, greater resistance to disease and high wind, and more receptivity to fertilizer and intensive care, Ho (1978:58–59) stressed that "science alone cannot transform agriculture without certain rural institutions being created first or at least concomitantly" and credited district agriculture improvement stations applying the findings of the Taiwan Agricultural Research Institute, both institutions established by the earlier Japanese colonial government. In the following decades many national and international incentives to change were offered to rural Taiwanese. Increasing the number of landholders and decreasing the size of landholdings were only two changes among many. Between 1951 and 1960, 10 percent of the growth in agricultural output resulted from increases in crop areas, according to Ho (155).

For the subsequent decades Fei, Ranis, and Kuo (1979:314–15) considered "land reform, followed by increases in multicropping and cultivation of new crops by the poorer (smaller) farmers, caused agricultural income to become significantly more equally distributed over time," but contended that land reform was not the primary cause of greater family income equity in rural Taiwan:

> Because nonagricultural income was more equally distributed than agricultural income, the growth of rural industries and services made a substantial contribution to FID [family income distribution equity]. . . . The steady increase of opportunities in rural by-employment available to members of rural families, especially the poorer ones, greatly contributed to the complementarity of growth and FID.[3]

Samuel Ho (1978:161) showed that the increases in productivity and income in the late 1950s were nearly as much as those in the early 1950s. Moreover, although the annual rate of growth in agricultural production was 4.6 percent during the 1950s, it was 4.1 percent during the 1960s and had been 4 percent under the Japanese between 1923 and 1937 (155). This long-term trend argues against the importance of a causal relationship between land reform and the putative effect of increased productivity.

Hidden taxes, in particular the government's fertilizer monopoly, and the official undervaluation of the price of rice in contrast to the market price transfer agricultural surpluses to other economic sectors. Landholders raising other crops had to purchase rice at market prices to pay land taxes, then had to sell it at the official lower rate, and to buy fertilizer at rates set by the Food Bureau (that is, the fertilizer monopoly). This is part of what Gates (1997:20–29, 206–21) aptly called the "tributary mode of production." In the ROC instance the Chinese ethnic oligarchy squeezed rice from the Taiwanese farmers and redistributed it to the advantage of Mainlanders on the state's huge payroll of Chinese hangers-on.

An additional turn of the screw on farmers not mentioned in the literature but familiar to rural natives is that farmer association officials, popularly known as "rice worms" (*bi-tháng*), after requiring the rice accepted to be of exceptional dryness, add water and then sell the "surplus" between the quota and the rehydrated weight for their own profit. B. Gallin (1966:77) noted the concern about rice being rejected for being too wet but did not mention that the standard of dryness is considerably less than universalistic or constant, especially varying depending on whether officials are acquiring or passing on rice.

The systematic government extractions of rice at valuations below market prices significantly hampered the possibility of families improving their standard of living by agricultural production and "effectively transferred part of the increase out of agriculture" to industry (C.-M. Hou 1978:132; also see B. Gallin 1966:76–79; H.-H. Hsiao 1981, 1990:67–94; S.-M. Huang 1981). Ho noted that productivity growth was negative during the late 1960s, "when land ceased to be added to that already cultivated." Overall, he attributed "the principal source of agricultural growth since 1951 [to] the more intensive use of current nonfarm inputs, especially chemicals and imported feeds (155).

The longer-term (1900–1960, interrupted by the chaos of initial KMT occupation) trend of increased agricultural productivity does not appear to have been affected by the land reforms of 1949 and 1953. Implementation of these policies clearly reduced rural inequality. Ho estimates that the price set for compensating expropriated landlords (2.5 annual yields) was less than half the market value prior to these policies. Moreover,

> by forcing landlords to accept bonds as payment, there was an additional redistribution effect, because they were in effect being forced to lend to the government a sizable sum of money at a real rate of interest [4 percent] substantially below the real current market rate [between 30 and 50 percent per annum]. . . . Most landowners who received stocks of government enterprises regarded them as an inferior form of asset. Consequently, many of them quickly liquidated part or all of the shares paid to them at substantial losses. Koo (1968:44–48, 156–57) estimates that landowners retained only between 4.5 and 9.3 percent of the shares of the Taiwan Cement Company (the most preferred of the government enterprises). . . . Depending on the stock the sale price was between 36 and 106 percent of par value. (Ho 1978:166–67)

That land—the most valued possession in Taiwan in 1953, or in "traditional Chinese culture"—was surrendered by large and small landlords with no significant opposition must be put in the context of the massacres of 1947, the "White Terror" that continued for years thereafter, and the continued activities of the secret police before drawing any conclusions about "the consent of the governed."

Barred de jure from accumulating land and excluded de facto from all but the lowliest government positions, Taiwanese aspiring to improve their standard of living had to emigrate or become entrepreneurs. Tenant farmers acquired land at a very good price and were able to increase their incomes faster than if they had continued to pay rent. Nonagricultural work, however, yielded still higher returns. Seeing the disincentives of growing rice and the incentives for industrialization, "the majority of young adults entering the labor force [since the mid-1960s] have gone into manufacturing or other nonfarm jobs" (Speare, Liu, and Tsay 1988:83). After lagging farther and farther behind other sectors of the economy, during the late 1980s farmers organized to protest the many policies that extract agricultural wealth to support industry, the huge army, and the bureaucracy of the Republic of China. Brutal police attacks on farmer demonstrations occurred in Daiba in 1988. Taiwanese anthropologists documented both the movement and attempts to suppress it during the twilight of the Chiang Dynasty (summarized in Hsiao 1990).

CHAPTER 7

# American Anthropologists Looking through Taiwan to See "Traditional" China, 1950–1990

Japanese and Chinese anthropologists working on Taiwan prior to the 1950s studied the aboriginal enclaves in the mountains of Taiwan or on smaller neighboring islands. Bernard and Rita Gallin (1974b) recalled that they found sociologists at National Taiwan University, not anthropologists, interested in their work during their first trips (during the late 1950s and early 1960s) to do fieldwork in rural Taiwan. Arthur Wolf (1985:3) similarly recalled that, into the 1960s, "Chinese and foreign anthropologists studying Taiwan practiced a strict division of labor. The Chinese studied the aborigines, and the foreigners studied the Chinese [from the context it is clear that this meant Taiwanese, not refugees from the KMT defeat in China]. The two groups exchanged reprints and dinner invitations, but when they went to the field they went in different directions to study different problems."

American anthropological work has focused almost exclusively on rural Hokkien (Holo) and Hakka speakers, although "Taiwanese" includes those of Austronesian descent (which, to some degree, most Taiwanese are) and those of the children of those born in China who arrived during the late 1940s. There is a great deal of anthropological literature, if hardly any in English, on aboriginal tribespeople, [1] scarcely any on Mainlanders' children who identify themselves as Taiwanese. Our review of representations by American social scientists recapitulates the concentration on Holo and Hakka speakers but is not intended as endorsing the narrowing of the category "Taiwanese" to exclude anyone born on Taiwan who identifies as Taiwanese from this category.

### Arthur Wolf and the Unthinkability of Taiwanese

Arthur Wolf was one of the first American social scientists to do fieldwork in rural Taiwan. His publications and those of the wife of his early fieldwork on Taiwan are the most frequently cited anthropological work dealing with

Taiwan and have considerable recognition outside East Asian/West Pacific studies. Having found what he was not originally looking for—a predominance of "minor marriages" in the southwestern portion of the Daiba (Taipei) Basin—he related his research on the implications of this phenomenon to a wider audience of social scientists than those interested in East Asia or in Pacific islands such as Taiwan. The high levels of daughters-in-law adopted at early ages (*simbû'a*) and of uxorilocal residence, which Wolf and others found to have been very common in northern Taiwan (41 and 15 percent, respectively), do not fit with the norms for the "traditional patriarchal Chinese family" at all (as Wolf and Huang [1980:125, 318] acknowledged; also see Pasternak 1989). The high rate of uxorilocal marriage should not have come as a surprise, however, to anyone familiar with the scant literature about Taiwan that was then available in English, since George W. Barclay, in *Colonial Development and Population in Taiwan* (1954:228–29), had reported that 15 to 20 percent of Taiwanese marriages between 1906 and 1930 were uxorilocal.

Division of household assets (*pun ke-hoe*) during the lifetime of the father would seem to constitute another anomaly to "traditional China."[2] Such patterns, though later attenuated, would seem to evidence important cultural differences between "traditional Taiwan" of the first four and a half decades of the twentieth century and mainland traditional China.[3] That these patterns anomalous to patriarchal Chinese family structure have been the central focus of Wolf's work makes his practice of promoting a view of a single Chinese essence all the more startling (to those unacquainted with the investment of the regime that welcomed Wolf to work with archival documents had in being the preserved "Chinese tradition").

Wolf, who continues to find the records of the Japanese Empire the best place to study traditional (imperial) China, asserted that only historians "still insist on treating China as though it had the internal consistency of rice pudding" (1985:15). Although, in this passage and elsewhere, Wolf seems to acknowledge diversity, it is always within a singular "Chinese society" or a singular "Chinese culture." Also, since he and his students deploy a single one of the Chinese languages, Beijinghua, his statement that "most anthropologists are now convinced that Chinese society is as varied in expression as the Chinese language" may concede very little. For that matter, rice pudding is often not homogeneous and does not merely blend together its diverse ingredients but frequently includes (unassimilated alien) elements like raisins that remain distinct from the rice. Despite Wolf's nominal recognition of diversity, his practice is one of relentless analysis of *Chinese society* in the singular.

Data from Taiwan are at least the major ingredient when not the only source of Wolf's data. Yet, invariably, singular nouns modified by *Chinese* and not *Taiwanese* appear in Wolf's titles, even though he recurrently acknowledged that the data from Taiwan may not be representative of Chinese sociocultural patterns. For instance, "Considering the source of most of the original data we are presenting, this book might appropriately have been entitled *Marriage and Adoption in Rural Haishan.* We chose *Marriage and Adoption in China* because we believe our argument has implications for the study of Chinese domestic organization generally, not because we view Hai-shan as representative of China" (Wolf and Huang 1980:ix–x). In that Wolf and Huang marshal data from various areas of Taiwan, not just from Haishan, "Marriage and Adoption in Taiwan" or "Marriage and Adoption in Japanese-Ruled Taiwan" would have been more precise. Modesty in claiming generalizability somehow just never makes it into Wolf's titles, although his students sometime skip to the local level in theirs (for example, "Religion and Ritual in Lukang" [De Glopper 1974]). "Taiwanese society," "Taiwanese culture," and "Taiwanese family" are literally unthinkable to Wolf and to some of his students.

In his contribution to *The Anthropology of Taiwanese Society* (Ahern and Gates 1981) Wolf covered "domestic organization." He brought himself to use *Taiwanese* six times—in contrast to twenty-five *Chinese* and *Hakka* or *Hokkien* seven times. Even in a volume manifestly about Taiwan, he used the phrase *Chinese family* exclusively. Wolf and other anthropologists writing about religion based on field materials from Taiwan end up with gods, ghosts, and ancestors and/or Buddhism, Confucianism, Daoism, animism, and perhaps Christianity as "Chinese religion," which remains in the singular, as in *Religion and Ritual in Chinese Society* (Wolf 1974).

A contrasting treatment by anthropologists of multiple religious realities is provided by Thailand. Even though, unlike Taiwan, Thailand has a state religion (Theravada Buddhism) that the king has special obligations to protect, as Herbert Phillips (1973:71) noted, there are "four internally consistent and clear, but different belief systems—Buddhism, Brahmanism, [4] a Thai version of traditional Southeast Asian Animism, and simple naturalistic explanations—each of which has certain explanatory functions, but which villagers (often the same individual) also use interchangeably and inconsistently." Even A. T. Kirsch (1977:241–66), who sees a functional division of labor between religious traditions in Thailand and some systematicness to alternation and syncretism there, distinguishes historical strata and divergent types of religion. No one speaks of an entity, "*the* Thai religion," in the singular. A similar unconcern for theological

distinctions typifies syncretic Japanese religious beliefs and practices [5]—
and even American "popular religion." As Donald De Glopper, (1974:44)
wrote, "There is no more reason to expect various Taiwanese customs or
beliefs to form a coherent, logically consistent, and uniform system than
there is to expect the doctrine of the Trinity, the tooth fairy, and Easter
eggs to fit together into a consistent 'American popular religion.' "

If four "world religions" and a widespread "folk religion" do not suffice
to trigger the plural *Chinese religions*, it is unlikely that *Chinese societies* can
be conceived, especially by those whose research has been sponsored, fa-
cilitated, or merely permitted by the "Republic of China" government. It
had its own reasons for maintaining a view that there is only China and
pretending that the government that happens to be located on Taiwan
should be recognized as the legitimate singular *China*, since it clearly did
not give proportional representation to those whom it actually ruled. A separate entity called Taiwan was not at all "good to think" for them. Indeed,
"Taiwan" remains a dangerous thought for the KMT (and various parties
led by former KMT members), even now.

That a concept "Taiwan" is so unthinkable to the most-cited anthropologist who has done fieldwork on Taiwan makes one wonder what danger
it constitutes for him, why it was not "good to think" for him. Fear of
losing access to data seems a likely possibility for someone relying heavily
on government archives. In recent decades loss of access to the means
of production of data is a salient concern for anthropologists, not just
in Taiwan. Fieldworkers unpalatable to the regime were denied entry to
Taiwan by the KMT/ROC government, just as were native Taiwanese (such as
KH) who criticized the government while studying outside Taiwan. American anthropologists familiar with Taiwan cannot be unaware of the KMT's
restriction of access. As Hill Gates (1987:240) put it:

> Where we can do fieldwork, our researches are constrained by tight
> governmental limits on the pursuit of topics that might undermine na-
> tional policy. Where we can not do fieldwork, we can do anthropology
> only on the safely dead. Intellectual issues thus come to be defined
> conservatively, and research topics become studies in the art of the
> possible.

Arthur Wolf has done both: not only has he avoided thinking or writing
"Taiwanese culture," but he has concentrated on the safely dead, writing
about "traditional China" on the basis of Japanese colonial records. [6] The
Japanese population records, covering two generations, have been widely
used by American social scientists to examine demographic changes. The

massiveness of these archives has been taken as prima facie proof of the validity of the records, as if, because there is so much, it *must* be accurate. With Wolf's confidence in the homogeneity of Chinese culture, he did not even consider the possibility that there might be variability among Taiwanese by class or by locale in their understandings of *ge* (family), in writing:

> The Japanese settled on the *chia* [*ge*] as the basic unit and wisely left it up to the natives to define the term. All that was required of people was that they register as members of one and only one *chia.* Thus we may be confident that the family preserved in these records is a product of Chinese customs and not an arbitrary creation of the Japanese colonial bureaucracy. (A. Wolf 1985:31–32; also see Wolf and Huang 1980, chap. 2)

Although he does not consider that Taiwanese may have manipulated definitions and registrations for their own purposes, he at least acknowledged a bias in the records against joint families: "They followed Japanese custom in designating the head of the household. When a head died or retired the headship passed to his eldest sons regardless of whether or not the family included the former head's brothers. Since the Japanese must have known that Chinese custom favors brothers over sons, my guess is that primogeniture was introduced as a clerical convenience" (A. Wolf 1985:33). Other biases or invalidities Wolf did not discuss. Yet in the major mid-1950s survey of community studies in Japan itself Richard Beardsley (1954) cautioned against accepting abundant official records as transparent:

> This method, though particularly enticing in Japan where any government office has a wealth of statistics on many different subjects, has very serious limitations, since many statistics touch on matters of taxation and government control, on which the government statistics collector finds it almost impossible to learn the true state of affairs. Careful check of the records against independent surveys of land ownership, occupation, and population in the small communities studied in the Inland Sea has invariably shown discrepancies; sometimes, indeed, the figures bear very slight resemblance to reality. (44–45)

If the detailed statistics for Japan itself are unreliable, there is little reason to suppose that similar statistics collected in other languages by Japanese officials in a colony are obviously valid or reliable. Huang Chieh-shan, who spent a decade working for Wolf on data from the registries,

*Complicity with Domination*

contended that they were more reliable than records from Japan because of the tighter police control on Taiwan than in the homeland or in Korea—or China of any dynasty (1989 interview). The lack of usable registration data from China is strong evidence that the institution was imperial Japanese, *not* imperial Chinese. There has been little (if any) concern about the procedures and motivations of those recording in or reporting to population registries, although M. Brown (2001, 2004) has shown systematic bias in the household registries' recording of ethnic classification and intermarriage rates. Studies on the ethnography of official record collection (for example, the locus classicus, Kitsuse and Cicourel 1963) are apparently unknown to those working on the demography of Japanese colonial Taiwan. Wolf once wrote that, "given that the Japanese household registers are the best source of evidence we will ever have for studying family composition in late traditional China, one of our research priorities must be to discover how people interpreted the term 'family' when registering with the Japanese police" (A. Wolf 1985:12). He has not, however, published work bearing on this research priority.[7] It will soon be too late to ask any Taiwanese who reported on their households to Japanese officials about their understandings of requirements and categories for registering household members.

In his preface to Huang's and his magnum opus, Wolf (1980:viii) claimed that the Japanese "household registers allowed me to determine the precise composition of every family from 1905 through the end of the Japanese occupation in 1945." Who it was in the "family" who decided whom to include as being part of it, by what criteria, and for what purposes are not problematics addressed within Wolf's work on the colonial Japanese archives.

Asking about responses made to Japanese police is "salvage anthropology" that is not being done and soon will be undoable, but researchers could ask similar questions about registering with the KMT police now. We know from the Gallins' research on emigrants from the Jianghua village that they call "Xin Xing" that some longtime residents in Daiba continue to be registered back in the village (1974a:344–46; the disparity between actual residence and registration was already noted during his 1958 fieldwork and reported in B. Gallin 1966:34–35). On the basis of censuses of two Daidiong (Taichung) villages conducted by students from Dunghai University, Mark Thelin (1977) found that the ROC household registries overcounted households, undercounted the number of persons within the households, and suggested motivations relating to taxation for household members to misreport to the official records.[8] Similarly, Tang Mei-Chun

(1978:179–83) reported that, in comparing official registrations with a 1969 census of a town that has been engulfed by Daiba, the existence of households and the kinship relationships of those within households were consciously misrepresented. As in the village studied by Thelin, even in the aggregate, Yellow Rock households were overcounted, although there were under-registrations as well as over-registrations. Less socially prestigious kinship relations (including the one that was Arthur Wolf's long-term focus, *simbû'a* and matrilocally resident couples, plus illegitimate children) and occupations were systematically misrepresented. Other systematic biases in the registers remain to be explored. Given that these registers bear such a weight in the study of "late imperial China" (and, coincidentally, for the study of colonial Taiwan), we can only hope that someone pays attention to the research priority suggested but ignored in practice by Arthur Wolf.

Within the Japanese colonial data set, if Wolf and Huang's data are disaggregated (by year as well as by place), we might be able to see that, even within the half-century of Japanese rule on Taiwan, in addition to considerable regional differences within Taiwan, there may have been temporal differences, so that the social structure (marriage patterns) in even Wolf's microcosm (Haishan) of the timeless essence "China" was changing, as had been reported (by Barclay 1954:228–29) before the Wolfs first went to Taiwan (also see Pasternak 1989:105–6). A. Wolf (in Wolf and Huang 1980:viii) acknowledged that "changes initiated by the Japanese occupation began to have significant effects" about 1930. Wolf's coauthor (Huang, 1989 interview) stressed that increased literacy undercut paternal authority, making it possible for sons to refuse to marry girls who had been adopted for future marriage. Bernard Gallin (1966:165) also mentioned "increasingly open opposition of young people" but stressed that an increasing ratio of females to males and improved financial conditions made brides "both easier to find and easier to afford." In arguing for the essential unity of a singular China (despite linguistic differences between southeastern provinces and the nonacceptance of foot binding among the Hakka whom he studied in Taiwan), Cohen (1990:123) adduced the use of Qing dynastic dates in account books in southern Taiwan for five years after the transfer of Taiwan to Japan as evidence of the hegemony of the (dubiously Chinese) celestial emperors. Five years to change something so fundamental to business practice and everyday thinking as dating seems rapid to us and a better argument for Japanese imperial hegemony as early as 1900. (Besides having a different standard for communist hegemony in China and Chinese hegemony in Taiwan, Cohen appears not to

*Complicity with Domination*

understand *hegemony*, since he can write that "hegemony in modern China received no commonly accepted legitimization through culture" (130).

## Folk Religion

Over time, as American anthropologists came to view "kinship" as a less-than-transparent or intersubjective category (see Wallace and Atkins 1960; Schneider 1968), the initial focus of anthropological research on Taiwan shifted from kinship and lineage organization to religion, usually with an implicit or explicit assumption that "traditional Chinese religion" had been preserved on Taiwan (and had been successfully extirpated by the communist rulers of China). Researchers on world religions found on Taiwan often have been oblivious to folk religion being a marker of eth-nicity in Taiwan. Participation in Taiwanese festivals has long been scorned by those born in China as "backward superstition." The ethnic minority governments (Manchu, Japanese, and Chinese) recurrently attempted to suppress, or at least limit, the frequency, duration, and expenditure on festivals derogated by Mainlanders as only one step removed from the extravagant goings-on of barbarian headhunters.[9]

The pantheon of a "Chinese religion" held in contempt by the ruling Chinese minority on Taiwan and by their Beijinghua-speaking offspring is supposed by some specialist researchers (prominently among them, Arthur Wolf) as mirroring a real political structure. In the Durkheimian tradition cognitive structures in general, and religion in particular, are reflections of society. Indeed, it is society that is worshipped in Durkheim's view. As Wolf (1974:8) put it, "It is clear that the peasant's conception of the supernatural world was molded by his vision of society." In the anthro-pology of religion on Taiwan, however, it is an earthly power that never exercised effective control on Taiwan and which surrendered responsibility for Taiwan more than a century ago—that is, a political order that is beyond the recall of anyone living on Taiwan. As Arthur Wolf's (then-) future wife, Hill Gates Rohsenow (1975:488), wrote, not just Taiwan but the areas of southeast China from which settlers derived "were largely on their own for a significant part of the later Qing dynasty. . . . It is paradoxical that the [current] iconography derives from an otiose and powerless dynasty several generations past, while the authoritarian and all-pervading present governments are rarely alluded to in its symbolism."

To say, as Wolf (1974:8) did, that "the supernatural world is never a simple projection of the contemporary world" is to put it very mildly.[10] It is no doubt salutary to "begin the study of Chinese [or of Taiwanese, a level of analysis between the village and China that never seems to occur to Wolf as a possible one] religion with the social and economic history of particular communities," but will careful local history explain the relevance of an extinct social order never particularly salient in the region (northwestern Taiwan) about which Wolf and others write? "To understand the beliefs held at any point in time, one must examine the history of the community as well as the contemporary situation" (9). Wolf continued, but, just as his demographic work is focused on the Japanese period, what he and his associates have written about religion tends to ignore contemporary situations in general, and ethnic domination in Taiwan in particular. As Rohsenow (1973a:479) wrote: "The struggles of the present are brushed over very lightly. . . . What events of contemporary life keep century-old animosities alive? . . . An analysis which attempts to show the relationship between religious symbols and social organization should make clear the nature of the social relations the ritual sphere is purported to express."

Some other anthropologists have seen religion as a potential expression of rural ethnic protest, although even they put *Chinese* rather than *Taiwanese* in the titles of works dealing with data from Taiwanese history and contemporary culture (for example, Weller 1987). As Bernard Gallin (1985:55–56) suggested, "The proliferation of religious activity in Taiwan and increased importance of the supernatural might be viewed as a nativistic movement to mark and enhance Taiwanese identity—as opposed to the Mainlanders . . . [who] are openly disdainful of what they refer to as Taiwanese superstition."[11]

Even Myron Cohen (1990:132) eventually wrote that what he called "traditional Chinese culture on Taiwan became very much transformed into a modern assertion of national identity, but in this case the identity was Taiwanese and the nationalism was linked to the movement for Taiwan's independence." The primordial/ethnic basis of self-identifying as "Taiwanese" has declined as children and grandchildren of the post–World War II influx from China have lived their entire lives on Taiwan and increasingly intermarried and become bi- (or multi-) lingual. That is, self-identification as "Taiwanese" is increasingly oriented to the hoped-for future of democracy and prosperity rather than to the rampant injustices of the KMT arrival, slaughter, and persecution of the majority population by a privileged and newly arrived Chinese minority (see Corcuff 2002; Chu 2000; Ho and Liu 2002). Nonetheless, credence in and support of temples predating the imposition of Chinese misrule continue to distinguish Taiwanese from Chinese.

*Complicity with Domination*

## Historical Sources of Taiwanese Invisibility
## in American Anthropological Discourse

Some American academics (for example, Mendel 1970; Lo 1994) have studied movements for Taiwanese independence, but anthropologists have not (even when venturing to research social movements on Taiwan [for example, Weller 2000]). Despite the well-known exemplary studies of nativist resurgence by Anthony F. C. Wallace (1956, 1970, 2003),[12] American anthropologists have largely avoided investigation of the resurgence of Taiwanese religion and its connection to Taiwanese struggles for self-determination. Given that American social scientists are generally liberal and that anthropologists dote on cultural differences, one would expect most of them to be sympathetic to self-determination and cultural maintenance anywhere—in Taiwan as much as in Slovakia, in Tibet as much as in Zuni. American social scientists marching in lockstep with a right-wing dictatorship legitimating—rather than treating skeptically—an ideological construct so shaky as "Taiwan is **the** most traditional part of China" is a puzzle. Although such a representation is overdetermined, we can suggest several partial explanations of how this status quo came about.

First, the triumph of the "People's Army of Liberation" on mainland China was traumatic for American China experts—not as traumatic as for the KMT but still traumatic. First General Patrick Hurley and then right-wing congressmen blamed the "loss of China" to communism on the China experts who had warned of the popular hatred of the KMT in China, as if observers were responsible for the reality they observed.[13] Shooting the messenger carrying bad news is a venerable reaction to frustration about military and political outcomes.

A second component to the acquiescence of American social scientists with the representation of Taiwan as typically Chinese is that the Maoist state made research inside China impossible—just at the time when anthropologists were beginning serious study of peasants and post-peasants (see chap. 2),[14] and just when there were some Americans with the linguistic means to do ethnography in Beijinghua (Mandarin), and just when some studies of communities on mainland China by Chinese natives were becoming available (Fei 1939; Fei and Chang 1945; M. Yang 1945; Hsu 1948; Lin 1948).

Robert Redfield abandoned plans for fieldwork in China. A few Sinologist anthropologists, who would later become prominent, started fieldwork in China between 1945 and 1950. Morton Fried did fieldwork in China after the war in an area still controlled by the KMT, though not where the Beijinghua he had studied was spoken. Having had to leave Sichuan without his fieldnotes in 1950, G. William Skinner did fieldwork among Chinese in Thailand for his (1954) doctoral thesis. During the 1950s no one had yet noticed Taiwan was the place where Chinese culture was best preserved. **Taiwan had not yet become the most traditional part of China.** In the 1953 American Anthropological Association memoir dealing with China (Wright 1953), there is no mention of Taiwan (or Formosa). Similarly, what would soon be represented as the most traditional part of China was unmentioned in Karl Wittfogel's *Oriental Despotism* (1957), although he included analysis of places such as Bali and southwestern United States pueblos that are farther from China and usual senses of *Oriental.* Those who wanted to study Chinese culture where Mao had not blocked them during the early and mid-1950s went to Southeast Asia, not to long-colonized Taiwan or Hong Kong.

Along with the first generation of researchers who began fieldwork in Taiwan in the late 1950s and early 1960s (Myron Cohen, Norma Diamond, Bernard and Rita Gallin, Burton Pasternak, Arthur and Margery Wolf), Skinner and Fried taught many of those who later did fieldwork in Taiwan. When their students began their fieldwork, they were preoccupied with finding continuities with what their teachers thought of as "Chinese" and had studied in China (Gates 1987:237). A later series of conferences, which led to Stanford University Press collections during the 1960s and 1970s, that were viewed by James Watson (1976:364) as "provid[ing] the very substance upon which Sinological anthropology depends for its corporate identity," "foster[ed] a generally conservative tendency to assume Chinese continuities over time and space," as Gates (1987:238) charged.

Researchers who wanted to study China were welcomed by a government pretending to be China. Moreover, being open to foreigners—whether social scientists or businessmen—at the time that KMT state capitalism was changing to encourage foreign investors—helped demonstrate that there was a "free China," in contrast to the larger, but closed, Maoist China. Writing in English about a timeless, essentialized Chinese culture and society in Taiwan was the safest kind of free speech for a regime that until the end of the 1990s restricted other kinds of discourse—especially any discourse about ethnic differences and Taiwanese autonomy. In return, social scientists were grateful for a chance to study at least something they could label "Chinese" in their publications (thereby getting more attention for them).

The KMT was eager to facilitate research legitimating its view of reality, arranging access to archives, forcing cooperation from village officials, providing assistants, and even some financing of research by Americans. Hill Gates noted that

> the Nationalist [KMT] need for legitimacy caused them to emphasize cultural continuities with China. . . . Often writing in English, and clearly for an American audience, Nationalist supporters in Taiwan and the United States based many of their arguments on the premise that Taiwan was an integral part of China, and its people were wholly and essentially Chinese. (1987:232)

Wishful thinking on the part of those who wanted to study China dovetailed with the need of a government claiming to represent all China but not sufficiently secure of its legitimacy as a minority in the only territory it controlled to drop martial law for four decades. Social scientists who sought the legitimacy of being experts on "the world's oldest continuous civilization" or the world's most populous country shared the KMT interest in claiming that "traditional China" had been preserved by caretakers of the Japanese colonial regime for a half-century on Taiwan to provide foreign observers a sort of Ming theme park. For instance, Taiwan is a particularly good setting for comparative work, according to Baity (1975:2), because "the Chinese live there as an overwhelming majority of the population, govern themselves[!] according to more or less traditional Chinese principles, and are relatively free of the influences of a present or former colonial power." The fantasy that the Japanese were caretakers of "traditional Chinese society" is explicit in the introduction to *The Anthropology of Taiwanese Society*:

> Taiwan is the only province of China that has not undergone the sweeping changes of a socialist revolution: Chinese life has greater continuity with the past there, it can be argued, than anywhere else. During fifty years of rule, the Japanese did not intentionally alter Chinese customs and social relations; subsequently, the Kuomintang [KMT] government actively promoted adherence to Confucian ideals of social order. Anthropologists have therefore gone to Taiwan to study what they could no longer study in other provinces. It was Taiwan's representativeness, not its special qualities, that first attracted their interest. (Gates and Ahern 1981:8) [15]

Just to call Taiwan a "province of China" is to take a stand with the KMT and against the right of self-government of the people on Taiwan. Moreover, *province of China* has little historical warrant. Until 1886 Taiwan was a territory of the province of Fujian, although Qing forces controlled only one-third of the island's land mass (Chuang 1988). The Japanese did not classify Taiwan as a "province." While Chen Yi was looting the island after World War II and while the KMT still controlled some territory on the Asian continent, Taiwan was not considered a province. Within the fantasy "Republic of China" Taiwan contains three provinces. Thus, in the four-plus millennia of Chinese civilization(s), Taiwan was considered a "province of China" only for seven years before the Qing Dynasty unloaded what its chief negotiator with the Japanese (Li Hongzhang) regarded as a bleeding ulcer on the motherland. Before the Chinese government transferred its claim to sovereignty over Taiwan to Japan, the dangerous frontier outpost was certainly *not* considered typically "Chinese."[16]

In combing the literature on Taiwan, we have not encountered any nineteenth-century claims that Taiwan was the most representative part of China or the best place to understand Chinese culture and society. It is hard to imagine anyone seriously believing that Japanese imperialism made Taiwan more Chinese instead of more Japanese. If a half-century of Japanese rule is "a bridge to the past," as Gates and Ahern (1981:9) characterized it,[17] it is quite an unusual assumption that colonial rule that introduced universal education—conducted in Japanese, not in any Chinese language, and aiming to assimilate (*dôka*) Taiwanese as Japanese (see Ching 2001)—"pacified" the aboriginal population of Taiwan so that peasants could concentrate on agriculture and forget about defense, presided over the demographic transformation from an island with the death rate equivalent to the birthrate to one with the birthrate double the death rate (Tauber 1974:362), and also built a network of roads and railroads that markedly increased the access of the countryside to production for export (see Grajdanzev 1942; Ho 1978; Barrett and Whyte 1982) somehow simply *preserved* "traditional culture."

Generally, production for export is considered an indication of "modernization." As a Japanese colony, Taiwan was integrated into the world economy more than any part of mainland China was. An early "green revolution" made it far more productive than any part of mainland China was (or is). Nowhere else in the world is integration into the world economy taken as an indication of wholesale "preserving tradition." Those who want to study traditional Chinese culture on Taiwan ignored that the "bridge to the past" was a Japanese bridge to the past—and, once on the other side, had to ignore the influence of the Dutch East Indies Company recruiting, sponsoring, and supervising the Hakka- and Hokkien-speaking men leaving their lineages behind in southeastern China to clear land and grow crops for export. Of course, in the view of those who wish to find traditional Chinese culture, neither the European supervisors nor the aboriginal Formosan tribes they fought and with whom the migrants intermarried were of any cultural importance. Having gladly transferred claims on Taiwan to Japan, Li Hongzhang (1913) wrote:

> Formosans are neither of us nor with us, and we praise all the ancestors that this is so! In all Asia, in all the world, I believe there are no tribes of animals called men more degraded and filthy than these people of Taiwan. And have we not enough of criminals and low creatures to deal with on the mainland? These people are not farmers, they are no hill-men, nor hunters of wild beasts whose skins bring in money and keep men's bodies warm in the cold winters. No, they are not even fit to be soldiers in trained armies, for they have no discipline, nor could they be taught. Neither would they make good sailors on regular ships though many of the coastmen are good enough as wild pirates and buccaneers of the sea. They are cut-throats, all of them, along the coasts and back into the jungles. And so they have been from the days of Chia-Ch'ing to the present time. No, they are not all even of so good a class as that! For what are opium smokers, head-hunters, and filthy lepers. . . . A very large number of these people are opium users of the lowest kind, and those who do not use this hellish concoction only abstain from it because it is not within their power or means to obtain that dirtiest of evil drugs. (268)

This late Qing official did not anticipate that anyone would claim that Ming culture was transported wholesale to Taiwan in the final years of the Ming Dynasty and there alone lived on through the Qing Dynasty and beyond. In 1895 the island was viewed as unimportant to China and as quite abhorrently *un-Chinese*.

If, rather than efforts of seventeenth-century European or twentieth-century Japanese curators of Chinese culture, it was the retreat of the remnants of the KMT army to Taiwan that made Taiwan the most representative or traditional part of China, one might expect that anthropologists would have studied the Mainlanders, using their memories to reconstruct what Chinese life was like before 1931 (when Japan invaded Manchuria), much as Native Americans told the first two generations of professional American anthropologists about pre-reservation life. Although the KMT supporters who fled to Taiwan constitute a quite unrepresentative sample of the population of China, at least they grew up in China and had not been socialized within the Japanese Empire. Insofar as there has been "salvage anthropology" on Taiwan, however, it has concerned either the aboriginal

Formosans or research in the Japanese archives. Studies of the "memory culture" of China, akin to the classic works of Yang and Lin, have not been encouraged or elicited from Mainlanders resident on Taiwan by American social scientists (or by their Chinese and Taiwanese students). As already noted, American social scientists, beginning in the late 1920s, preferred studying functioning cultures to eliciting recollections and sorting through them to compare "culture elements." The functioning culture of units small enough to be studied in a year or so of fieldwork was Taiwanese villages, not the urban enclaves of exiled Mainlanders, despite the urban focus of Fried's and Skinner's work.[18]

One particularly striking failure of anthropologists on Taiwan is to look at what Mainlanders did about forming lineages when they were separated from their natal lineages during the late 1940s and were dwelling in a hostile frontier area dominating, but outnumbered by, natives. A great deal of early work, especially by Columbia-trained anthropologists, dealt with the conditions of lineage formation in the eighteenth and nineteenth centuries on Taiwan, but this interest did not extend to seeking to observe this feature of Chinese culture among contemporary Mainlanders in protracted exile on Taiwan. It is also odd that the "sojourner" conceptualization—developed by "Chicago school" sociologists to account for Chinese in North America who planned to return to China (P. Siu 1952, 1987[1953])—has not been applied to studying Mainlanders on Taiwan. (In both cases most "sojourns" lasted the rest of the sojourners' lives.)

Although there has been some painstakingly systematic work on Japanese archives and other government records, another characteristic of an early age of faith in cultural homogeneity and easy access to it continues. As Fried (1954:24) noted in his review of community studies done on mainland China:

> since the subjects of anthropological research in the past were almost invariably [treated as/conceived to be?] of a simple homogeneous nature, there was little need for the field worker to concern himself with the source of his information, other than to be reasonably certain that he was not relying too heavily on the reports of people who were recognized within their own culture as being markedly deviant.[19]

Anyone, in any place—Indonesia, Malaysia, Singapore, Thailand—would do for eliciting *Chinese culture*. Who needed sampling if communities and individuals were interchangeable and *Chinese culture* static and homogeneous? Sampling is not one of the strengths of American anthropology

*Complicity with Domination*

and was even less so in the 1950s, when intracultural variance was grappled with by only a few anthropologists.[20]

Gates suggested a third, related basis for studying Taiwan as a surrogate for rural China—not Ming or Qing China but the China in which a communist peasant revolution had just triumphed—in order to try to understand conditions leading to that revolution, and to look for possible ways to prevent other, similar revolutions:

> By the late 1950s it was clear that American anthropological fieldworkers would not be welcome in the People's Republic of China for the foreseeable future. It was beginning to appear too that the McCarthyist destruction of China scholarship in the United State was hampering the American ability to understand events in China proper. Support [from foundations] emerged for anthropological investigation of everyday Chinese life in Taiwan, where, it was assumed, traditional Chinese culture had been preserved from the changes set in motion by the Communist revolution. . . . The anthropological literature contains a marked bias toward seeing Taiwan as a sample of an essentially homogeneous Chinese whole. (Gates 1987:236, 232)

It would have to be admitted that Taiwan would have been an excellent place to study the KMT officials and army who "lost China," as well as to monitor their tactics, after retreating there to ensure that they were not pushed further east—that is, into the sea. Following the massive wartime effort to develop expertise about the areas in which American troops were fighting or in which the government anticipated military action and/or postwar occupation, and preceding the counterinsurgency research such as Project Camelot, the 1950s was a boom time for area studies. The "Truman doctrine," and its enthusiastic extension by Eisenhower's secretary of state, John Foster Dulles, made it the responsibility of the United States of America to save that world from communism, which seemed seductively attractive to peasants. Whether land reform and rural reconstruction might halt the "Red Tide" was an important policy question even before the escalation of American military presence in Southeast Asia led to grasping for the "hearts and minds" of peasants suffering through a guerrilla war there. Although land reform would seem patently "un-American," given the importance of land speculation and large landholdings in U.S. history and current agricultural production, it does seem to have been approved and even prescribed for other parts of the world, in particular during the military occupation of Japan.

A fourth factor in explaining why American social scientists looked through Taiwanese culture without seeing it is a general problem of "Orientalism." Edward Said, who is a member of another group that was politically invisible until very recently to Americans, wrote a comprehensive critique of Western research on the Middle East. As he wrote, the "Orient" has

> a kind of extrareal, phenomenologically reduced status that puts it out of reach of everyone except the Western expert. From the beginning of Western speculation about the Orient, the one thing the Orient could not do was to represent itself. Evidence of the Orient was credible only after it had passed through and been made firm by the Orientalist's refining fire. The Orient is eternal, uniform, and incapable of defining itself; therefore it is assumed that a highly generalized and systematic vocabulary for describing the Orient from a Western standpoint is inevitable and even scientifically "objective." (1978:283, 301)

With the substitution of *China* and *Sinologist* for *Orient* and *Orientalist,* these (and much else of his critique) applies directly to the fabrication of a singular Chinese culture.

Said noted that, in the study of Arabic, Indian, Chinese, and even Japanese culture, Western scholars were preoccupied with a glorious, classical past as preserved in old texts, rather than in making sense of the messy, living present. He noted a general flight from the disorientation of direct encounters with living carriers of a culture to the safety and manageability of documents. One does not expect to encounter this pattern among anthropologists, but it does seem to occur among some who work on civilizations with long written traditions. Reading American Sinologists, one feels that they want to skip over not only the Japanese occupation of Taiwan and of northeastern China but the whole Manchu period, to reach back to Ming China.[21] Said shows that the positing of timeless entities such as "Chinese society" is a recurring habit. The most distinguished comparativist sociologists interested in China—Wolfram Eberhard, Max Weber, and Karl Wittfogel—often treated materials from different millennia as part of a single, static Chinese society. For Taiwan Japanese and KMT household registration records, rather than ancient literature and court records, provide the escape of preference from complicated contemporary realities to documents. Murphy (1982:39) provided two apt analogies to the standard operating procedures of Sinology: this literature is like what Asians might write about Europeans "if they felt obliged to avoid the confusion of referring to Germans, French, and Italians as different peoples . . . [and] as if

Asian scholars were explaining current European attitudes by reference to material from the early Roman Empire."

Into the 1960s, if "primitives" were not available for study (and after a half-century of Japanese rule, the Formosan aboriginal cultures could not be so classified even by those eager to ignore any changes in Hakka and Holo cultures on Taiwan), then anthropologists studied peasants. In either case the

> classical manner in ethnography may be summarised thus: It is assumed that within a somewhat arbitrary geographical area a social system exists; the population involved in this social system is one culture; the social system is uniform. Hence the anthropologist can choose for himself [or herself] a locality of any convenient size and examine in detail what goes on in this particular locality. He then generalises from these conclusions and writes a book about the organisation of the society considered as a whole. (Leach 1964:60; see Barth 1993:171–73)

Although the "whole" for work on Taiwan is often "China," this was not the case of ethnography done in China prior to the victory of the "People's Liberation Army" in 1949. In the community studies done in China before any Western community studies in Taiwan—with the telling exception of Francis Hsu's study of non-Han villagers in the Chinese periphery of Yunnan (Hsu 1948)[22]—there was "little tendency to overstate the significance of the results in terms of the area to which they applied. Indeed, most of the authors leaned the other way, inserting a prominent caveat that the community described is not China but an aspect of a huge and diversified society" (Fried 1954:22).

Moreover, there was also a thoroughgoing critique in American anthropology of *village* as a "natural unit" of analysis for peasant societies (see Geertz 1959; and, for China, Skinner 1964). Again, Bernard Gallin showed another, better way: *Hsin Hsing, Taiwan* was exemplary in stressing that "Hsin Hsing and the other villages of the immediate area are far from being small, isolated units" (1966:45). This pioneer study of a Taiwanese village aimed to describe change, not an incarnation of that timeless essence, the *traditional Chinese village*. Although change was not the problematic of her community study, Norma Diamond (1969:2) was also careful to point out that the Dailam (Tainan County) fishing village she studied in the early 1960s had been "subjected to modernizing influences for some 60 years [and so] it should not be mistaken for a picture of traditional China."

In trying to understand why some American anthropologists writing

Table 1. Country(ies) Listed in Titles of Books and Articles Reporting Research on Taiwan by American-Trained Anthropologists by Institution of Their Doctoral Training

| Training University | Percentage of Publications with | | | |
| --- | --- | --- | --- | --- |
| | Only *China** | *China* Primary† | *Taiwan* Primary‡ | (N) |
| Berkeley | 78 | 0 | 22 | (9) |
| Washington | 67 | 0 | 33 | (6) |
| Columbia | 64 | 14 | 22 | (36) |
| Stanford | 55 | 4 | 41 | (22) |
| Harvard | 50 | 0 | 50 | (8) |
| Cornell | 41 | 9 | 50 | (54) |
| Other** | 19 | 9 | 72 | (68) |
| Johns Hopkins and Michigan | 18 | 9 | 73 | (11) |
| Michigan State | 0 | 20 | 80 | (10) |
| Total | 39 | 9 | 52 | (223) |

\**China* or *Chinese* in title, without *Taiwan* or *Taiwanese* in title or subtitle.

†*China* or *Chinese* in title, with *Taiwan* or *Taiwanses* in title or subtitle.

‡*Taiwan* or *Taiwanese* in title, with *China* or *Chinese* in subtitle or in niether title nor subtitle.

\*\*Universities whose almuni published fewer than five publications based on research in Taiwan are combined as "Other."

$x^2 = 53.2$, 18 d.f., p < 0001

about Taiwan have followed Hsu rather than the other early writers of Chinese community studies in claiming "the typicality of his population and equat[ing] it without major reservation to a generalized traditional Chinese norm" (22; also see 19–20), perhaps the key is precisely that Taiwan and Yunnan are peripheral areas with strong historical non-Chinese influences as well as being under KMT martial law at the time Hsu and the other ethnographers were working in these places.[23]

Nonetheless, there are also works closer to the Taiwanese ground. In effect, there is intracultural variation within American anthropology. The Taiwanese basis of research is more readily visible in the titles of books and articles by anthropologists not trained at Berkeley and Columbia, as can be seen in table 1.

There is no diminution over time of Taiwanese invisibility in American anthropological work done on Taiwan. Indeed, there is a slight (though statistically nonsignificant) **increase** in Taiwanese invisibility in the titles. Early book-length American ethnographies of Taiwan (for example, Bernard Gallin's *Hsin Hsing, Taiwan* and Norma Diamond's *K'un Shen; A Taiwan*

*Complicity with Domination*

*Table 2.* Taiwanese Visibility by Topic in Publications by American-Trained Anthropologists*

| Topic | Only *China*† | *China* Primary | *Taiwan* Primary | (N) |
|---|---|---|---|---|
| | Percentage of Publications with | | | |
| Medicine | 62 | 0 | 38 | (13) |
| Family/Kinship | 51 | 9 | 40 | (23) |
| Religion | 54 | 0 | 46 | (85) |
| Other | 28 | 8 | 64 | (85) |
| Women | 18 | 6 | 76 | (17) |
| Total | 39 | 9 | 52 | (223) |

*Publications *without* Chinese, China, Taiwanese, *or* Taiwan *in the title.*
†*Includes four titles with* Taiwan *or* Taiwanese *and* China *or* Chinese *in subtitle.*
$x^2 = 29.2$, 8 d.f., $p = .001$

*Village*) included *Taiwan* in their titles—in English, at least.[24] Before producing the string of titles with *Chinese*, even Arthur Wolf entitled his 1964 dissertation "Marriage and Adoption in a Hokkien Village."

There are, however, also (statistically significant) differences by topic of research. As shown in table 2, research on kinship and religion especially evidences participation of American anthropologists in the imposition of traditional China on Taiwan. Research on ethnomedicine and research about working women is by no means unconcerned with the "great tradition" of Chinese civilization but has generally contained closer attention to Taiwanese distinctiveness. In addition to professional socialization, some places in keeping the Taiwanese location out of titles, significant variation can be accounted for by whether research was done in Daiba Guan (Taipei County) or farther from the capital.

Using stepwise regression of a dichotomous dependent variable of whether *Taiwan* or *Taiwanese* occurred in the titles of 223 books and articles based on fieldwork in Taiwan by American-trained anthropologists published before Lee Tenghui's first election, we found that training at Columbia University, the University of Washington, or the University of California, Berkeley, in contrast to training at institutions other than these three to be the best explanatory variable. Research topics involving kinship, medicine, religion versus other topics, and research in Daiba Guan versus elsewhere also had statistically significant effects. Betas were .37, .23, and .20, respectively. The same three variables were the only ones accounting for significant variance in *China/Chinese* receiving primacy in the title (whether or not *Taiwan* was also visible there), with betas of .37,

.24 and .14, respectively. The multiple *R*s were .46 and .43, respectively. In addition to interaction effects of the variables with statistically significant correlations to the two specifications of the dependent variable, year of publication, book versus article, and alternate combinations of topic were included in the analysis but did not have statistically significant effects. Still, the positive effect for year of publication (indicating increasing Taiwanese invisibility) makes dubious the claims that there was a widening sensitivity to essentializing a monolithic Chinese culture and greater restraint exercised before American ethnographers moved on to the PRC.

Gates and Ahern (1981:7) claimed that anthropologists "develop an instinct for telling if a book with 'China' in its title deals with Taiwan, Hong Kong, the PRC, or the T'ang dynasty." Other than by recognizing the authors on the basis of their earlier work, it is unlikely that this supposed "instinct" develops. Indeed, for a previously unfamiliar American anthropologist's publications, it is necessary to look into the book or article to find out if it is based on research done in Taiwan. Even then, especially in Ahern's work, it is sometimes difficult to tell apart assertions that are generalized from Taiwan to China from those based on mainland Chinese sources. Moreover, it was not always necessary to depend on developing such an instinct to know whether a publication described Taiwan.

## Ethnomedicine

The study of folk medicine blossomed on Taiwan during the 1970s. Although more likely than research on other topics to have *Chinese* rather than *Taiwanese* in titles, unlike the more or less contemporaneous work on "Chinese religion," the medical anthropology literature based on fieldwork done on Taiwan were more likely to record native terms in whichever language was used by healers and their clients, rather than imposing Mandarin ones. Most of the illustrative material in Arthur Kleinman's very widely influential 1980 book, *Patients and Healers in the Context of Culture,* was from Taiwan.[25] In addition to establishing explanatory models of illness rather than of disease as the proper focus of medical anthropology, that book made Taiwan the exemplary case of medical pluralism. The families of sick Taiwanese do not merely "doctor shop" but (often in succession) pragmatically try healers from different medical traditions. These include Western medicine, with its focus on microorganisms (viruses and bacteria) and its often high-tech remedies; Chinese medicine (*diong-i*), with its humoral etiological theory and herbal remedies; geomancy (*hong-sui*) providing insights into problems resulting from improper alignment of houses or tombs; and Taiwanese spirit mediums (*dang-gi*) exploring illnesses caused by ancestors and other spirits, who must be palliated in order for the ill person to recover. Each kind of practitioner offers explanations of what went wrong to bring about illness as well as attempting to provide remedies for the presented problem. Some of the remedies work in some cases, and some of the explanations are accepted. However, there is considerable variance in the attribution of which treatment was efficacious (not even temporal contiguity, that is, the remedy closest in time to recovery, is an adequate predictor of which medical belief system will be substantiated by the illness trajectory), and the standards in everyday use for confirming the validity of diagnosis are also quite elastic.

In contrast to analyses of "Chinese religion" in the singular on Taiwan, medical anthropological work done on Taiwan during the 1970s stressed the pragmatic diversity in medical behavior and intracultural variation in the salience and content of medical beliefs. Bernard Gallin (1975:277) cautioned against inferring commitment to a medical tradition (that is, assuming that what is tried is salient to those—not necessarily the "patient"[26]—who decide to try some kind of healing): "Utilization of the traditional systems does not necessarily imply belief in these forms of medicine. Many people 'go through the motions' "—just as they do in the realm of religious rituals. As he had described "Hsin Hsing" villagers earlier, "not even the most skeptical are entirely convinced that the rituals are ineffectual" (Gallin 1966:264). Gallin (1975:278) also cautioned: "We must be more careful not to attribute the same knowledge, perceptions, and behavior to all member of Chinese society[/ies]. For too long, we took for granted the universality of the knowledge and even the behavioral manifestations of the tenets of the great Confucian tradition among the Chinese population[s]."

De Glopper put it even more bluntly:

> There is no single, pristine Great Tradition of Chinese medicine. There are several distinct schools, and when you look at what actual practitioners are doing, the variety is even greater. . . . Since people commonly utilize several therapies at the same time, it seems hard to assume that they are strongly motivated by a desire for conceptual consistency or a single language with which to experience their illness. . . . They do not place their entire confidence in any single practitioner, whether MD, traditional doctor, diviner, or spirit medium. In my experience on Taiwan a tendency to keep one's options open and to prefer multi-causal explanations is common among ordinary people,

as is an appreciation of the unique qualities of a very particular case or event. What cured one may not cure another, or what cured someone at a particular time may not work later, because the circumstances are different. (1977:264)

In contrast to the situation in other research specialties, Taiwanese culture is visible and recognized in medical anthropology work. This does not mean that the anthropologists had any particular interest in Taiwanese (medical) culture. As in other specialties, fieldwork shifted from Taiwan to China when researchers could go there at the end of the decade (with Kleinman again in the lead). Nevertheless, they did not posit a consistent, overarching entity, "Chinese medicine," for comparison with "Western medicine."[27] The data on local and individual diversity in medical belief systems in retrospect might seem unmistakable, but anthropologists have demonstrated a considerable capacity for ignoring intracultural variation in presenting models of this or that culture. Moreover, during the same period "Chinese religion" remained an authoritative construct, despite data of similar pluralism in religious practices from Taiwan.

One partial explanation for the difference between these research specialties is that the typically Orientalist fascination with texts was markedly lower in the work on medicine on Taiwan than in the work on religion, despite the huge corpus of Chinese texts in various medical traditions.

Another reason for the difference in visibility of Taiwanese materials is that medical anthropologists were much more concerned with ethnosemantics than were anthropologists writing about Chinese religion[28] and were therefore more leery about translating native terms into Beijinghua.[29]

Furthermore, although medical specialists were certainly a focus of attention for medical anthropologists, religious specialists, particularly Daoist priests, were more central in the anthropological discourse about religion in research done on Taiwan. That is, the behavior and beliefs of those mixing or successively using divergent medical technologies received more attention than the structured behaviors and beliefs of the expert professional practitioners. Medical anthropology was and is more concerned with messy, varying practices; the anthropology of religion tends to construct clean-cut, neat cosmologies with little consideration of the variability of knowledge of the cosmology or in the credence of particular beliefs.[30]

One "messy" Taiwanese practice in particular, viewed with considerable distaste by Chinese Mainlanders on Taiwan, spirit possession, was a central concern of anthropology during the 1970s (see Lewis 1971; Samarin 1972;

Bourguignon 1973; Fry 1976), although for research locales other than Taiwan it tended to be considered in the domain "religion" rather than the domain "medicine." The lack of possessed healers in central and northern China has led to other problematics emerging from fieldwork there—and to a lack of comparison to what was studied on Taiwan during the 1970s. Nonetheless, due to the centrality of Kleinman's 1980 book to a paradigm shift within medical anthropology, the diversity and complexity of Taiwanese reality was unusually visible in that research specialty, and not just the specifically East Asian/West Pacific work within it.

The recognition of Taiwanese (culture and language) within medical anthropology of the late 1970s and early 1980s was more apparent than real. During that same period (the last burst of anthropological work on Taiwan before Western anthropologists were welcome in the PRC), there was one subspecialty of American anthropology that clearly examined Taiwanese patterns without subsuming them in *Chinese tradition* or *Chinese society*.

### Working Women: The Exception to the
### Pattern of Finding Traditional China on Taiwan

The wide distribution of industrial enterprises to the countryside of Taiwan attracted the interest of many social science observers. Elsewhere, industrialization was an urban phenomenon. Landless workers from the countryside migrated to urban centers. During the first Industrial Revolution in Europe only mines and lumber mills—both processing raw materials where they were—blighted the countryside. Otherwise, the "dark satanic mills" were located in cities. Noting the rising standard of living in Taiwan, many observers were euphoric, considering Taiwan as a model for rural industrialization without urban social problems. The widespread pollution of the environment went all but unrecorded in the enthusiasm for an example of "spatially equitable" economic development.[31]

The exception to this euphoria was some feminists (Linda Arrigo, Norma Diamond, Rita Gallin, Hill Gates, Lydia Kung) who studied women working in urban and rural factories and who saw and remarked that small family enterprises were practically unregulated in terms of worker safety and treatment. They also noted that Taiwanese women constituted a reserve labor army, by postponing marriage and childbirth, much as had the poor families who sold their labor in nineteenth-century British factories. Taiwanese women constituted

> a submissive, docile, and transient labor force, willing to accept low pay and unlikely to remain in one job long enough to agitate for wage

increases or improved working conditions. With their minimal training, they are also prepared to accept the lackluster and poorly paid jobs available in labor-intensive industries. . . . To ensure sustained production at low cost during periods of economic growth and political stability during periods of economic recession, the Taiwanese [*sic*][32] government encourages an ideological environment that relegates women to menial labor and household tasks. The marriage of patriarchal ideology and contemporary capitalism allows the family, the nation, and the international market economy to take advantage of women's unpaid domestic and underpaid public labor without altering cultural definitions of male and female roles or transforming the structure of male status and authority within the family. (R. Gallin 1984:397–98)

Most of the unmarried young women's earnings were turned over to parents, who often invested this income in the education of sons. Diamond (1979) reported that women factory workers who lived with their natal families gave 70 to 80 percent of their earnings to their parents. Those moving farther away and living in factory dormitories also remitted nearly half of their earnings. Diamond and other anthropologists and sociologists who did fieldwork among women factory workers on Taiwan during its industrialization did not find substantial increases in the independence of these women from decisions made about their lives by men. For the most part the young women maintained traditional views about the appropriateness of female subordination (see Gallin 1984:396; and Diamond 1979), although attitudinal surveys reported Taiwanese men and women stating that women have increasing or equal say in decisions about expenditures (Yang 1970:449). The economic importance of daughters has increased with marriage postponement. Stafford (1992) showed reassessment of investment in daughters as they take increasing responsibility for ancestor worship and funding family investments of other sorts.

At least through the 1970s factory work was a station at which many young women "repaid" parents the cost of raising them prior to marriage (and the benefit of the family into which they passed). The median age of females leaving employment (ca. 1972) was 29 (Speare et al. 1988:103). With no prospects for advancement within the workplace and with widespread discrimination against the employment of married women, factory discipline was succeeded by subordination to a husband for women who worked for wages until marrying. The relatively short-term involvement in the labor force, in turn, has been used to justify not promoting women who are viewed as "fickle" and/or "will just get married

*Complicity with Domination*

and leave anyway"—a rationalization not unknown in the United States. The criticism of the exploitation of women factory workers as a reserve of labor to be used or let go with fluctuations in business cycles, and to be routinely exposed to toxic materials in unsafe working conditions, is the exception to widespread celebration by American social scientists of the "Taiwan miracle" (for example, Kuo et al. 1981; Gold 1986; Clark 1989). This insulting-to-Taiwanese locution is embedded in discourse on political economy arguing against "dependency theory" (for example, Winckler and Greenhalgh 1988; and Gates 1987:50–67). It is also an important exception to subsuming *Taiwanese* under the rubric *Chinese*.

With shortages of labor during the 1980s and early 1990s, the pattern changed, and, according to official statistics, "in 1986 52% of Taiwan's female employees were 30 years of age and older; 42% were married" (R. Gallin 1989:374). These statistics raise questions about the continued application of analyses of working Taiwanese women during the early 1970s. The "reserve" may have been "called to active duty," and/or the demands for more skilled labor have made workers less interchangeable, as also in South Korea (see Cho 1989:469).

Research on Taiwanese working women remains an exception to the conception of shared, traditional, Confucian Chinese worship of whomever has power that is advocated by the ROC government and exemplified by researchers whom it supported and was supported by.


### Conclusion

Social scientists have too often supported—in their words, in their presences, and in their deeds—the paternalistic claims of rulers suppressing the very cultures the anthropologists want to study. Social science work dealing with Taiwan routinely legitimated substitution of the language of Beijing for the language used by those observed and justified ignoring Taiwanese culture by subordinating consideration of its specific features to writing about Chinese civilization, just as Taiwanese were economically and politically subordinated to the fictitious "Republic of China." The "China" that Arthur Wolf and others serve in return for support of their research on what purports to be China is an egregious, but unfortunately not unique, example (see Asad 1973; Winks 1987:43–51).

The following two chapters examine the best-known and most widely diffused anthropological writings from the 1990s based on fieldwork from Taiwan (albeit presenting field materials gathered in 1960). Little new ethnographic fieldwork on the rapidly changing and democratizing Taiwan has been done, as American anthropologists flocked to work in the still autocratic society of the PRC, though at least one English anthropologist was supported by the KMT dinosaurs (Chiang Ching-Kuo and Luce foundations and delivered new work done on Taiwan under the guise of *Chinese* [Stafford 1995]).

# PART III

Anthropological Writing of the 1990s
Based on Research on Taiwan

# CHAPTER 8

# A Taiwanese Woman Who Became a Spirit Medium

## *Native and Alien Models of How Taiwanese Identify Spirit Possession*

On the side of the village opposite my (Keelung Hong's) natal home a man considered to be a *dang-gi* frequently went into a trance and sounded as if he was possessed by Mahzo (Matsu), the maternal protectress most worshipped by Taiwanese (see Ng 1988; Tsuah 1989). I grew up taking for granted that some people go into trances and that people seek advice about health and other concerns from gods and goddesses speaking through borrowed bodies—in voices distinct from the everyday voices of those they possess. (In the case of the man across the village the voice seemed very high-pitched and feminine when he was possessed, in contrast to his normal speaking voice.)

Until the late-1980s I was certain that, unpredictable and positively capricious as deities are, they would never choose to occupy so unclean a vehicle as a woman's body. Of the three bases for considering women "polluted" that Ahern (1978) extrapolated from Taiwan to "Chinese culture,"[1] it is the production of menstrual blood that I thought would make it impossible for a woman between the ages of menarche and menopause to preside in a temple or to provide a suitable vehicle for a celestial being to borrow.

The dangerous power women have to alter a family's form by adding members to it, dividing it, and disturbing male authority (Ahern 1978:276) —amply illustrated by Margery Wolf (1968, 1972)—is not particularly relevant to possession. The third source of "pollutingness," low social status, also seems of little relevance, since the pre-possession social status of male *dang-gis* is generally also low.

Despite the fit between my sense of my culture's logic and the nonnative professional anthropologists', my inference that women cannot be female *dang-gis* was mistaken. Before reviewing the anthropological literature on Taiwanese spirit possession, I did not know that Tseng (1973) included a case study of a female *dang-gi* and that Jordan (1972) also mentioned one. I was quite surprised to learn that a woman seven years my junior literally across the road from my natal home had become a *dang-gi* and was regularly possessed by Mahzo.

In a now well-known analysis of "The Woman Who Didn't Become a Shaman" (originally published in the *American Ethnologist*) Wolf (1990, 1992) presented an outsider explanation of a woman who some Taiwanese villagers for a few days in March 1960 thought *might* be a *dang-gi*. After discussing the woman *dang-gi* from my village in more detail, I will review Wolf's analysis of why the woman in the village she called Peihotien was judged to be crazy and compare her with some of individuals whom instances Taiwanese recognize as *dang-gi*s. Using information in March 1960 field notes Wolf published in the expansion of her 1990 article into a 1992 book, I will present both an insider-believer model for recognizing genuine spirit possession and a nonbeliever model that is more consistent than Wolf's model is with what her probably Christian,[2] and strikingly unnamed,[3] research assistant recorded about the 1960 events and that is also consistent with the histories of the three *dang-gi*s best known to my family and to me. Having produced a more general and more credible model of plausibility criteria used both in my native village and in the Taiwanese village about which Wolf wrote, I will discuss why the *dang-gi* role spills out of the etic domain of "medicine," especially fee-for-service medicine. Finally, I will argue that a few days of uncertainty and contestation about a dubious instance does not evidence that there is no shared cultural model.

## The Woman Chosen by the Goddess

Li A-Koan was born with and retained the most common, and historically most dominant, surname in my village (Singong in Daidiong County), which had families with multiple surnames. Her father was the second son of a father who was a large landowner early in the twentieth century. At the time her father was drafted into the Imperial Japanese Army, he did not own any land. His elder brother inherited and squandered most of the land their father had before land reform (see chap. 6) could have redistributed any of it. A-Koan's father, Li Mun-Hiong, had a Taiwanese wife before entering the military. While stationed on the (Japanese-conquered) island of Hainan, he married a second wife, Li Mi-Yen, who came to the village with him several years after Japan surrendered its colony of Taiwan in 1945.

I remember that the second wife did not speak Holo very well when I was growing up. Angered by his preference for the "minor wife" (*se-i*) he had chosen for himself and who he considerably favored, his first (arranged) wife divorced him after Li A-Koan was born in 1950. Li Mi-Yen then was promoted to the full rank of wife. I remember (and my relatives have confirmed) that the couple did not have very much land and were exceptionally eager to make money. They bought gasoline from soldiers not authorized to sell it and resold it on the black market. They tried to manufacture cigarettes even though the government tobacco monopoly literally counted the number of tobacco plants of authorized growers and also undertook extensive surveillance of unauthorized plantings. Tobacco monopoly enforcers seized the Lis' illicit tobacco and cigarette-making paraphernalia several times. The Lis also learned to make a concoction to set women's hair, *den tau mun*, literally "preparation for electrically frying head-hair." This tended not just to "fry" users' hair but to burn their scalps. A somewhat dubious reputation—built by bringing back a foreign wife, not giving the first wife her due, and engaging in illegal (cigarette manufacture) and unsavory (dangerous hair-setting manufacture) attempts to make money—was capped by the manner of A-Koan's father's death. Li Mun-Hiong died a particularly gruesome death by methanol poisoning from drinking counterfeit Western liquor with a business associate.[4]

My youngest brother and his wife, who were A-Koan's classmates, recall nothing unusual about her as she was growing up. In particular, they could recall no indication from Li A-Koan of any special interest in worship and healing.

Like her mother before her, Li A-Koan married an alien soldier (in 1973).[5] I thought that he was from the mountainous eastern portion of Daidiong County (*guan*) and thereby closer (presumptively in proportion of blood as well as in propinquity) to the Polynesian aborigines (*wuan zu min*). He was, however, another kind of outsider, the son of a Hainanese friend of Li Mun-Hiong. The couple divorced in 1978, and Li A-Koan, then 28, returned to her widowed mother's home with her three young children.

Divorce remains uncommon in Taiwan, especially in the countryside (Farris 1989). Taiwanese spouses need not like each other, nor are they expected to continue sleeping together, but divorce is more of a last resort than it is in North America or Western Europe. That a father would relinquish sons is even more unusual. When divorce does occur in contemporary rural Taiwan, children—especially sons—remain in the husband's family. His brothers' wives and/or mother and aunts raise them. Reputedly, this father was wholly taken up with drinking and gambling—to such excess that both divorce and custody of the children by the mother was accepted.[6] That she is native to the village and that her husband marginal (Hainanese rather than Taiwanese) probably eased acceptance of her having custody.

I would not expect public criticism, but there does not even seem to have been censorious gossip directed at the wife who had taken the extreme steps (within the assumptions of Taiwanese culture, particularly the imperatives of ancestor worship) of divorcing a husband and taking with her "his" children. That she worked for remuneration (in a supermarket in the nearby town) is less unusual than divorce or child custody by the mother. Work outside the household is increasingly common, although less so in the countryside than in the cities (R. Gallin 1989).

Seeking to serve the gods is also uncommon. As in other cultures in which gods take over the bodies of people (see Besmer 1983; Bourguignon 1973, 1991a; Elliot 1955; Wafer 1991), Taiwanese accept the call to serve only with great reluctance—usually only after illness has convinced them that service is going to prolong their life that is fated otherwise soon to end. Although Li A-Koan is not regarded as having sought to become a *dang-gi*, Li Siu-Min, her brother, encouraged by their mother, came close to seeking to be possessed by the mother goddess.

Li Siu-Min dreamed the second Mahzo of Dua Do (a temple, also in Daidiong County) wanted him to take her home (in the form of a carving, *gim sin* [literally golden body]) and install her on his home altar (not in my village but in one nearby). Accompanied by his mother (and not by his sister), Li Siu-Min undertook a pilgrimage to Dua Do. His mother urged him to choose one of the black-faced Mahzos, but he resisted, since this was not the image of his dream. On a return visit Siu-Min found the right *gim sin*. He installed her on his altar and endeavored to go into a trance to receive the goddess. He was not able to do so, or, if he did, Mahzo did not choose to use her eager would-be son (*gi chu*).

One day his sister went to his house while he was seeking to become a vehicle for the goddess. Li A-Koan went into trance easily, and Mahzo began speaking through her, albeit quite softly. Being from Fujian, Mahzo, of course, speaks Holo (Fujienhua), the native language of most Taiwanese.[7]

After Li Siu-Bin had moved northeast to a predominantly Hakka town, Mahzo appeared to him in another dream, expressing displeasure with the noisy location of his (and thereby the goddess's) new house, between a highway and railroad tracks. Mahzo did not specify where she wanted to move. Siu-Bin chose to move her to his mother's house.[8] There Mahzo entered Li A-Koan regularly. Men and women, both from the village and from elsewhere, came to consult with the goddess. I was not able to obtain an estimate from A-Koan, A-Koan's family, or my own about whether locals or outsiders were more numerous in this. All were able to agree that the majority of the consultations related to health and that most occurred at night. Apparently, the goddess sometimes spoke through Li A-Koan even when she was not in a trance, although the answers the goddess gave through her in either condition were so softly spoken that it was hard for anyone to be sure what she had said.

A-Koan returned on an annual pilgrimage to renew her spiritual connection to the Dua Do temple from which her brother received the *gim sin*. Her mother told me that A-Koan abstained from eating meat on the first and fifteenth of each month and had only a simple, vegetarian breakfast each morning.[9]

### The Rareness of Challenges

No one to whom I talked about her in my natal village expressed any doubts about the genuineness of Li A-Koan's call. Nor had any *dang-gi*s or other Taiwanese experts been summoned to judge whether a god or a ghost was possessing her.

When I was growing up in the village—a time in which any agricultural surplus and more was extracted by the government, so that the cost of being in service to the gods exceeded any possible material gains—the village *dang-gi*'s vocation also was unchallenged. Once near the end of his life, however, while he was (in villagers' view) pretending to be possessed, he heard someone talking to his daughter-in-law and blurted out: "Give him the vegetables!" He was unable to convince villagers that the goddess had taken this interest in his household's finances in preference to the topic about which Mahzo was being consulted. Even this episode, however, did not lead to doubting that Mahzo had generally genuinely possessed him in earlier instances. At most it raised questions about whether he had lost the call/vocation near the end of his life, missing the specialness of a vocation that had lapsed, so that he started counterfeiting trances and reception of messages from the goddess.

Discussions of the genuineness of a call to serve occur, albeit infrequently: there is a reluctance to say with certainty that someone is faking possession. "Going through the motions" (B. Gallin 1975:277) may be more common than directly challenging possession (or the knowledge of "priests" and "doctors"), though such a formulation implies a greater skepticism than I think is operative.[10] There is nothing to gain, and much to risk, in denigrating a deity. Moreover, it is impossible to disprove (see Fidler 1993:221). Those who doubt the genuineness or efficacy of a god (or a *dang-gi*) go elsewhere, without expressing disrespect. Rural Taiwanese take a very laissez-faire attitude toward one another's beliefs. Publicly challenging other people's beliefs from the certainty of a singular Universal

Truth is un-Taiwanese. This is vividly obvious from the mix of Buddhist, Daoist, and imperial (Confucian) deities venerated in any temple as well as in the widespread credence given to animist explanations.

That someone is being possessed by a ghost rather than a god—and, therefore, needs the services of a *dang-gi* rather than being able to provide them—is a greater concern than that she or he is faking possession. From early on this was a concern of villagers in the case described by Wolf. Mrs. Tan's family called in a *dang-gi* with no local authority ("someone who had not been seen around here before" [65]). [11] His judgment did not close the case. A few days later, however, the regional expert Ong Hue-Ling (Hoe-Leng) visited Mrs. Tan. [12] His conclusion that she was "just crazy" was generally accepted—not just in deference to his expertise but from shared interpretation of Mrs. Tan's behavior while with him. The account that Wolf published in the *American Ethnologist* did not mention what Mrs. Tan did, but the fieldnotes included in her book (75–77) mention that several women called attention to Mrs. Tan having almost knocked Ong down in grabbing her husband and pulling him into the bedroom, saying she wanted "to be a bride" and to "have the first night of marriage" with him. This is wildly inappropriate behavior for an ostensible god—and only slightly more acceptable for a woman being visited by an esteemed elder.

Although both Li A-Koan and my family's *dang-gi* in Dailam consider themselves, respectively, the daughter of a goddess and the son of a god who possess their bodies when in a trance, they also consider themselves still part of their families when not in a trance. That is, they are not (as Wolf [1992:111–12] asserted) lost to their families. Rather, like the bride adding the husband's name at the time of marriage, the *dang-gi* gains an **additional** parent. The previous ones' authority is somewhat reduced—often on a regular schedule—but it is **not** eliminated. And there are secondary gains in the form of social esteem for the family, along with more tangible gifts from grateful followers. [13]

### Native and "Real" Explanations for Recognizing Divinities

I am well aware that native cognition is not the only object for anthropological study. Yet, however shaped it may be by the structural variables that aliens carry into the field with them and with which they claim to understand better than (in their view) benighted natives do, native cognition shapes decision-making in general and the acceptance or rejection of these women's possessions in particular. In understanding why Taiwanese villagers believed in Li's possession by a goddess and did not believe in

Tan's, native standards of plausibility *must* be considered, even by those who believe that such standards are determined by more "real" and abstractly universal explanatory variables, such as sex/gender and class, [14] that some anthropologists think natives are either unable or unwilling to see. Many anthropologists consider native models somewhere between epiphenomenal and inherently obfuscatory. [15] In this section I will show that explanations of gender and class that are readily apparent—even to outsiders, such as Wolf, who do not speak the local language [16]—do not explain the difference between Wolf's case and that of my childhood neighbor, and I will discuss some of the factors attended to by those raised in Holo-speaking rural Taiwan.

To those who live inside Holo Taiwanese ("traditional") culture, it is obvious that Li A-Koan was accepted as a *dang-gi* because a goddess—and not just any goddess but the most widely worshipped goddess on Taiwan— possessed her. Similarly, for insiders,[17] one reason that Mrs. Tan was not accepted as a *dang-gi* was because she was not possessed by any known god or goddess. As already noted, an established (though not locally known) *dang-gi*, possessed by the god whose image Mrs. Tan "bought,"[18] declared very early that Mrs. Tan had met a ghost (65, 96). Although that view was not universally accepted, when the region's expert rejected the possibility that she was possessed by a god (75–78), his judgment was based on evidence villagers considered compelling and had already been discussing before the definitive judgment confirmed it. Consensus followed very quickly.

Not crediting such male authority, and committed to serving as a witness of women's oppression,[19] while Wolf was unable (due to not speaking their language—in addition to her palpable contempt for such "superstitious" beliefs) directly to enter conversation with most village women about why they did or did not think Mrs. Tan was possessed by a god, Wolf's assistant (pseudonymized as Wu Chieh) gathered statements interpreting Mrs. Tan's behavior. However, neither the published fieldnotes nor analyses in Wolf (1992) contain any general discussion by villagers of what they considered criteria for recognizing *dang-gis*. Wolf did not attempt to learn Taiwanese plausibility criteria or ask her unnamed Holo-speaking assistant to elicit data on the question. She substituted an ad hoc set of social attributes, some of which positively correlated to being an accepted *dang-gi*, others of which are not even positively correlated, and only one of which is criterial for rural Holo-speaking Taiwanese.

As Ewing (1994:572) wrote, "To rule out the possibility of belief in another's reality is to encapsulate that reality and, thus, to impose implicitly the hegemony of one's own view of the world." Moreover, and of specific relevance to the present instance, Bourguignon (1991b:25) wrote, reporting of native beliefs "may be tainted both by the language and the beliefs of writers." Wolf (1992) exemplifies such dismissal by explicitly rejecting the possibility of the "default" Taiwanese view about possession by gods or by ghosts (that is, that they are real): "I did not entertain the presence of a god as one of the explanations of Mrs. Tan's behavior" (89). For her religious beliefs are entirely epiphenomenal reflexes of social categories (cf. DeGlopper 1995:239).

Generalizing from her own disbelief, Wolf also did not entertain the hypothesis that Peihotien villagers or Taiwanese *dang-gi*s believe in their gods either:

> [Mrs. Tan] had as many shamanistic characteristics as others who went on to full tang-ki status did. Her origins were humble; she was functionally illiterate; she was sincere, devout, and kind-hearted; she had led a harmless and unimportant life; she had a history of psychological breakdown that could be attributed to the god's attempt to make her into a vehicle; she had resisted as long as she could; she went into trances and spoke in a voice other than her own. (109)

Humble origins, functional illiteracy, sincerity, devoutness, and kind-heartedness typify millions of Taiwanese, particularly women, circa 1960. However, sincerity and kindheartedness are **not** attributes justified by Wolf's account of Mrs. Tan—in particular, her wrangles with her neighbors, whom she viewed as bullying her or her children; her persecution complex; and Mrs. Tan's own mother's assessment that she "is the kind of person who cannot get little things out of her mind" (63–64). Within the expectations for dutiful daughters that Wolf has written about extensively for more than a third of a century, Mrs. Tan had a history with two spectacular failures. An 11 March 1960 field note provided background from Mrs. Tan's mother: "I gave her to another family to be an adopted daughter."[20] This family "sent her out to be a cook or servant for another family. She didn't like this and something else happened,[21] and so she came running back to me. But I had to send her back to her adopted family" (63). Taiwanese (especially but not only women) are expected to *jia kho*, that is, keep eating whatever bitterness is their fate. One need not approve the expectations that a young woman would meet whatever demands are made on her by her adopted family and by the family to which she had been sent to serve to note that, in fleeing what very well may have been two intolerable situations, the future Mrs. Tan caused her natal family to lose face (which equals social "harm"). After her natal mother forced her to return to her adopted family, she behaved bizarrely enough to be sent back to her natal family, causing it further loss of face (for being rejected and, even more so, for being crazy) as well as having to expend maintenance costs on her.

The earlier break was known in Peihotien: a 5 March fieldnote reports that "someone told Wu Chieh that something like this had happened to 48 [Mrs. Tan] before" (62). If other Peihotien villagers did not know this then, they soon would have learned it. Moreover, besides having taken her to a mental hospital on 4 March, early on her husband had publicly announced that "she was probably going crazy 'again'" (94). On 12 March Wu Chieh overheard him "telling all the women that he knew that it wasn't true that a god was in her body" (66).

There is no evidence that Mrs. Tan, her mother, or anyone else interpreted the earlier breakdown as a god trying to take her over. That "this never happened again until now" (her mother, quoted on 63) demonstrates that the very widespread pattern of a spirit's demand to take over a body escalating in severity if refused was **not** instantiated by Mrs. Tan. Similarly, Wolf presents no history of attempts by Mrs. Tan to resist possession. Instead, she and her husband seem to have been quite eager to acquire the esteem of what Wolf calls "shamanhood" (100 and in her article's title), or at least to talk about it (66).

Although, as Lewis (1975:78–80) pointed out, the distinction between *shaman* and *spirit medium* often seems to depend on national tradition (Americans found shamans on both sides of the North Pacific, British found spirit mediums in Africa, and both generalized from those foundational locales), there **is** an analytical distinction possible between shamans controlling spirits and spirits controlling the mediums they possess (Firth 1959:141). Winkelman (1990) provides a systematic account of the differences, including beginning age (puberty vs. adulthood), volition (seeking to become a shaman vs. being seized involuntarily by spirits), social organization (hunting/gathering societies vs. agricultural societies with political integration above the level of local communities), explicit training of shamans, and occasional engagement by shamans in malevolent magics. Mrs. Tan was even less shamanlike than Taiwanese *dang-gis*, who generally schedule when they go into trances. Even such "control of the spirits" is minimal compared to Siberian shamans manipulating (even dominating) their spirit familiars (see Eliade 1951; Sternberg 1927; and, for more recent analyses of increasing female occupation of the role marginalized by Soviet campaigns, Balzer 1987, 1990). Appell and Appell (1993:55) cogently argue that "the term *possession* is culturally contaminated and compromised as a scientific term . . . [from condemnatory] Christian theology." *Medium* is only slightly less negatively loaded, albeit with less specifically Christian animus.

Wolf also mentioned several variances from expectations for *dang-gi* conduct, of which speaking "too often and too much about herself as Mrs. Tan rather than behaving as a vehicle who was unaware of her pronouncements while 'in trance'" (100) [22] is probably the most crucial for native skeptics. Her everyday (out-of-trance) behavior (specifically, her excessive behavior when her children got into fights (64), her husband's "crazy again" announcements, and whatever was known about her past all contributed to a "craziness" frame. Since Kleinman's (1980:214) definitive rejection of *dang-gi*s suffering major psychopathology, anthropologists have not claimed that the role of *dang-gi* is a niche for psychotics, as in the tradition of Kroeber (1940), Spiro (1967), and Sutlive (1992). Giles (1987) convincingly challenged the conventional wisdom about the psychological instability of those who are recurrently possessed even in the heartland for such theorizing, sub-Saharan Africa.

Wolf presents no evidence that if a man, say Mr. Tan, had behaved the same way he would have been accepted as a *dang-gi* by Taiwanese villagers. Indeed, she wrote that "even had Mrs. Tan been male, I suspect her legitimacy would have received closer scrutiny than that of most men in the village" (111), because the Tans were suspect "newcomers" who had been in the village less than ten years (95).

The contrast of the rejection of Mrs. Tan's possession and the acceptance of Li A-Koan's three decades later and roughly eighty kilometers farther south holds sex and gender of the "potential shaman" constant and facilitates examining some of the other components of Wolf's atheistic explanation of the case of Mrs. Tan.

I consider that gender did not differ, because both were devoted mothers, the main criterion for being considered an adult woman in Taiwan. Mrs. Tan had left two households, Li A-Koan one. Both thereby showed a fairly unusually high amount of independence from the ideal norms that require women to stay wherever fate puts them and to endure whatever suffering comes their way. I cannot imagine anyone contending that divorce or being returned by a family that adopted one makes a rural Taiwanese woman cease to be a woman (whether in sex or gender). Albeit not a very impressive one, Mrs. Tan had a husband in residence. Li had two visible brothers and a mother (a more than usually outsider one, it will be recalled). Neither one had a father around.

The "grand tradition" of Western social thought expects secularization to correlate with industrialization (both being part of "modernization"), so that the difference in time should operate against the later case. Moreover, improved sanitation and medical care since my youth, which was contemporaneous with Mrs. Tan's going crazy, have led to a healthier population with "less need for religious healing than previously," in David Jordan's (1994:148) estimation, and to "a shift in the proportion of Taiwan religion that is linked to physical illness." He quoted a villager explaining to him "in the mid-1970s that the village made little use of some of the new spirit mediums that I had seen initiated a decade before because 'things are more harmonious now than they used to be'" (149). That is, the market for *dang-gi* healing declined between when Mrs. Tan tried to enter it and when people in my natal village accepted Li A-Koan's vocation. In that Li A-Koan had a job, she participated more directly in the modern cash economy than Mrs. Tan had. (Gods and goddesses have not been reported to find women with incomes of their own favored vehicles.) Unlike Tan, Li was literate. Li and her village were more prosperous and aware of the world beyond the village than Tan and the village in which she lived in 1960. Both Chinese rulers and American atheistic rationalists expect such "modernization" (especially any embourgeoisement) to make possession **less** plausible.

Anthropologists have largely ignored whatever regional (and rural-urban) differences exist in Taiwanese beliefs and practices.[23] Wolf freely extrapolates to "Chinese culture" from her observations in northwestern Taiwan, so the relatively short distance between villages within the northwestern quarter of the island will be ignored here.

Although by no means a term with a single, agreed-upon definition/referent, *marginality* is ubiquitous in the cross-cultural discourse about spirit possession (for example, Lewis 1971; Bourguignon 1973, 1991a; Giles 1987; Atkinson 1992; Boddy 1994). Wolf repeatedly invoked it as crucial to the case of Mrs. Tan, especially stressing that the Tans were newcomers to the village of Peihotien. Although Wolf did not say that they were poorer than others were, she stressed the absence of a father and brother. Li A-Koan's father bore the most common surname in our village. Although not a newcomer, his long absence for foreign military service, his bringing back a foreign wife, their very dubious economic endeavors (trafficking in various illicit substances), and his horrifying death all distinguished him in undesirable ways from other villagers and made his children seem at least somewhat alien. Both Li and Tan were quite soft-spoken in everyday life, not notably self-assured or successful, as Wolf (111) asserts that *dang-gi*s generally are. My family's current male *dang-gi* and the male village *dang-gi* of my childhood could also be so characterized, so this does not

seem to distinguish Li and Tan from each other or from the male *dang-gis*
I know.

Both were deviant in breaking out of positions from which there is supposed to be no escape or return. Moreover, Mrs. Tan was heard repeatedly
to shout: "I don't want to live here" (67). Whether interpreted as a motivation or a secondary gain of her earlier breakdown, it did get her away
before—and would again. Taking sons away from a husband is more deviant than having servants or adopted daughters running away. Treatment
or diagnosis for mental illness is very stigmatizing (see Kleinman 1975,
1980), but, if *marginality* is equated with "craziness," a not very interesting
explanation that Mrs. Tan was judged as being crazy because she acted
and/or had a history of acting crazy would result. Presumably, Wolf meant
more than this. That there was no preexisting frame of "craziness" for Li
A-Koan is important in distinguishing how the two women were judged:
"Crazy or possessed?" is a question that did not come up about Li.

Perhaps most important, there was never any question about what deity was possessing Li A-Koan. Mahzo is a goddess with many worshippers
throughout Taiwan and one widely and locally known to possess *dang-
gis*, including our earlier village one. In contrast, Mrs. Tan purported to
be possessed by a new god: "We never did get a name for this god, who
needed a special paint job (with half his face black and half white) but still
looked and acted very much like [the village god] *Shang Ti Kung*" (Wolf
1990:429). *Shang Ti* (*Siong-Te*) is a generic appellation for a god in heaven
(commonly used for the single Christian god, for instance), not the name
of a specific Chinese or Taiwanese deity. Depending on what language
Wolf was romanizing, *kung* could either be an honorific (for example,
"grandfather") or the word for a god's "palace" (that is, a temple). Wolf was
either unable or unwilling to supply the Chinese character to disambiguate
her romanization when I wrote to ask her for it. Apparently, she not only
failed to get the name for the god Mrs. Tan claimed was possessing her but
did not get the specific name of the village god, either.

The appearance of a heretofore unknown god requires especially close
scrutiny. From the perspective of nonbelievers in possession, such a new
and unspecified god is "a much tougher sell." For believers it all but guarantees consideration that a ghost rather than a god is involved. No one
had to guess who was possessing Li A-Koan or search for the right *gim
sin*. Moreover, Li A-Koan's vocation was not rejected on her (annual) visits
to the Dua Do temple, as Mrs. Tan's was by the widely respected regional
expert.

It seems to me that, in the society of Taiwan in the 1990s that was more affluent (albeit at a high price in island-wide environmental degradation) than in 1960, Li A-Koan was as socially and economically marginal as Mrs. Tan. And, in having no husband, Li A-Koan was more socially marginal (living at home, but in a real sense disgraced). The social recognition of A-Koan's legitimate possession by a goddess and the social consensus that Mrs. Tan was not possessed by a god depend **not on differences in their status but on differences in their conduct,** in and out of trance, and on the reputation of the deities (venerated vs. unknown).

The efficacy of the god or goddess's proposed action and the accuracy of his or her predictions form an important part of how Taiwanese evaluate *dang-gis*. Mrs. Tan's calling was generally rejected before many predictions or remedies could be evaluated. Li A-Koan's growing following evidenced satisfaction with the results from consultations with the Mahzo who possessed her.

The contrast of these two cases strongly suggests that being a woman was less important to the rejection of Mrs. Tan as a *dang-gi* than Wolf claims. There are many more male *dang-gis* than female ones, now as in the 1960s.[24] It may be harder for a Taiwanese woman than for a Taiwanese man to be accepted as a *dang-gi*. Nonetheless, as the case of Li A-Koan, earlier documentation of Taiwanese female *dang-gis* (Jordan 1972; Tseng 1973), and the more recent studies by Nickerson (2001) and M. Brown (2003) show, being a woman was not necessarily a bar. The Taiwanese view is that the deities choose more male than female vehicles. Even if one takes Wolf's antagonistic view that people choose gods rather than that gods choose people, she provided no evidence that women's claims are rejected more than are men's. The relative proportions of *dang-gis* by sex cannot distinguish between fewer women making claims and women's claims being rejected more.

Like the orthodox Hindu analyzed by Shweder (1991:58), the Taiwanese follower of Mahzo "does not view his or her own ideas as arbitrary, conventional, or consensus-based, or as emotive expressions of imagination, desire, or will." The kind of explanation of individual motivations, status striving, and the focus on (human rather than divine) socialization that Wolf offered are typical of the literature on spirit possession (for example, Bourguignon 1991a:17, 23).[25] Consideration of such factors is not merely superfluous but dangerously hostile in the native view (Ewing 1994). To suggest that *dang-gis* are "trained"—that " 'job qualifications' are, obviously, derived from the observation of professional, experienced shamans" (107)—borders on blasphemy to believers, just as such a choice of labels is offensive and rejected by Pentecostalists who view their speaking in tongues as a result of being filled by the Holy Spirit, not as derived from study or from being taught (Samarin 1972:51, 55). In the view of believers, gods and goddesses know how to behave when they take over a body. They choose whomever they want, female or male. They do not justify or explain their choices. Humans are supposed to submit to their will, not to question their choices. If one looks at how Taiwanese **recognize** the gods' choices, the plausibility of divine explanations and the efficacy of prescribed remedies, along with clear discontinuity with the everyday self, are far more important than social scientists' transcendental categories such as gender and class—or medicine and religion.

### More than Healers, Less Mercenary than "Doctors"

As noted in chapter 7, Kleinman (1980) made Taiwanese something of the prototype of "doctor shopping." Taiwanese (rural and urban) do not just "doctor shop" or "healer shop." They search for patrons—including celestial ones—who will explain their problems and may choose to intervene on behalf of their followers or to suggest what the followers can do to change their fate and to avoid disasters or remedy problems. The gods and goddesses who possess their terrestrial adopted children frequently keep something close to regular office hours—hours that do not compete or interfere with the mundane work schedules of those children. (The *dang-gi* my family currently consults is possessed only on Saturday evenings.) The deities may supplement their "schedule," but rarely do they fail to appear where and when they are expected by an established *dang-gi*.

As Wolf noted, *dang-gi*s "must not charge money for their services, but it is assumed that reasonable gifts will be made by grateful clients" (107). Unfortunately, she followed the medical anthropology convention of calling followers "clients." Mainlanders and their children, who tend to be skeptical of anything Taiwanese, and especially what the KMT long dismissed as "superstitions" and tried to curb, may use *ke-ren*, but Taiwanese who are involved refer to themselves as followers (*sin-tô*), not as clients (in either language). However, reference to clients is irreverent to those so labeled. It is also part of forcing a role and belief system into the etic domain "medicine," obscuring the reality that "medicine" and "religion" are not distinct domains for Taiwanese who go to a *dang-gi*. More generally, "shamanism [in the generic sense that includes spirit mediums] is not in itself either a medical or a religious system; rather it is part of a comprehensive system of beliefs and practices relating the mundane human world to what is conceived to be a realm of the spirit" (Bernstein 1993:175).

## Insider/Outsider Analytical Criteria

In arguing that status variables are not criterial for distinguishing Taiwanese *dang-gi*s from non-*dang-gi*s, that the *dang-gi* role considerably overflows the category "medicine," and that Arthur and Margery Wolf have treated as "Chinese culture" roles (*dang-gi* and *simbû'a*) that both those on Taiwan who identify themselves as Chinese and those who identify themselves as Taiwanese consider especially "Taiwanese" and "un-Chinese," I challenge American anthropologists' categorizations. I am not contending that only a native can understand these things. If I thought that, it would be foolish to write in English attempting better to explain the *dang-gi* role and Taiwanese plausibility criteria for recognizing legitimate occupants of it.

Similarly, although I think that those who grow up in a place and who speak its language have an authority that short-term visitors who do not speak the language—and who rely on the reports in a colonial lingua franca in which they not fluent,[26] from assistants who are themselves outsiders to the village (and quite possibly hostile to native religion)—lack, I think that a sensitive alien **could** elicit through intermediaries what the criteria for distinguishing *dang-gi*s from non-*dang-gi*s are and see that Mrs. Tan's conduct did not meet the *dang-gi* criteria.

Wolf also signally failed to consider that there is a Taiwanese culture. In the best-known report of the fieldwork of which notice of Mrs. Tan's drama is a byproduct, Wolf (1968:vi) expressed her belief that

> China's history over the centuries has varied with the strength of its leaders, but its people have gone on being Chinese, whoever the ruler, whatever the political crises. I hope that . . . this study of an unimportant [Taiwanese] family may add to our understanding of what **being Chinese** is all about. (Emphasis added)

That book (*The House of Lim*) made many generalizations from an account of a Taiwanese family to "Chinese" customs and beliefs. To write that Taiwan is "just as Chinese as Peking is," Wolf (1972:viii) breaks with the views from both places and ignores the violence with which Chinese discriminated against Taiwanese, not least in the 1947 massacres. For Taiwanese, especially under martial law (1947–87), when other assertions of Taiwaneseness were repressed, *dang-gi* cults were seen both by Chinese and by Taiwanese as particularly "Taiwanese"—by the Chinese as symbols of our superstitious backwardness and by Taiwanese as symbols of pride in precisely those traditions derogated by our Chinese rulers, who attempted to "weed" them out.[27] Although focusing on what both Chinese and Taiwanese on Taiwan see as being particularly Taiwanese (adopted daughter marriage and spirit possession healing and counseling), what Arthur and Margery Wolf published from their fieldwork in Peihotien relentlessly labels its culture and religion "Chinese." Although reporting that she had stopped "feel[ing] comfortable speaking for Taiwanese women" after 1984 (in Rofel 2003:600), throughout her 1992 book (as elsewhere) she invariably used *Chinese* rather than *Taiwanese* to modify culture, society, marriage, patterns of thought, shamans, peasants, males, and females and reiterated her aim as being to "understand China" (4).[28] She also extrapolated quite different Singapore possession behavior (and, as the next chapter discusses, quite different Hong Kong naming patterns) to Taiwan. From my unsystematic observation of Taiwanese temples and families, rural-urban and north-south differences in reverence for *dang-gi*s are slight. In contrast, most of the "Chinese" on Taiwan (that is, those who arrived during the 1940s and many of their descendants) are contemptuous of *dang-gi*s. Indeed, contempt for *dang-gi*s is something of an ethnic marker for Mainlanders.

Even if distinctions made by Chinese and by Taiwanese in and out of Taiwan are unimportant to anthropologists, a mechanistic trait inventory analysis would show that neither *simbû'a* marriage nor a spirit possession complex are (or have been) typical across China, particularly not in the vicinity of Beijing nor in the central plains, the historic heartland of Chineseness. *Simbû'a* marriages like the one that was probably planned for the woman who became Mrs. Tan were not typical even across Taiwan but were concentrated in the northwestern part of the island, among Holo more than among Hakka speakers (Wolf and Huang 1980). Adopted-daughter marriage and spirit possession cults were not at all typical of pre-communist northern China, as is indicated by the use of the Holo terms (that is, *simbû'a* and *dang-gi*) even in the writings of anthropologists who generally translate "native terms" into Beijinghua in publishing in English. Within China, possessed spirit healers were concentrated in the southeast, from where overseas emigration from China (not just to Taiwan but to Southeast Asia and Indonesia) before the twentieth century mostly derived. The Confucian Chinese regime that ruled Taiwan until 2000 continuously propagandized against popular belief in *dang-gi*s. In common with other aspects of Taiwanese religion, cults of the deities possessing *dang-gi*s were seen by many Western anthropologists—including Ahern (1975), B. Gallin (1975), Kagan and Wasecha (1982), Kleinman (1980), and Weller (1987)—as expressions of Taiwanese identity in specific opposition to Chinese domination.

## A Last Filtering of the Bathwater

Given the magnitude of social and economic changes on Taiwan during my lifetime, the rejection of cultural change as explaining the different receptions of Mrs. Tan and Li A-Koan may have struck some readers as cavalier. Certainly, the expanse of space and time between the two cases is small in contrast to a great deal of writing about a singular transhistorical entity "Chinese culture" (regularly invoked and reproduced by Margery and Arthur Wolf), but I most certainly do not mean to suggest that cultural change is not occurring on Taiwan or that there is no intracultural (especially interethnic) variability.

Nor, by arguing that gender fails to explain the rejection of Mrs. Tan's divine possession, do I mean to suggest that gender is not an important variable generally (or, for that matter, in ways that Wolf missed, in the reception of Mrs. Tan's possible possession) or that Taiwanese women are or were treated or considered as equal by Taiwanese men. Employment of women in paid positions may soon be the norm for urban Taiwan—and is far from rare in rural areas. Although the cultural status of women has risen less rapidly than their income, both have risen. [29] Perhaps, women have become more plausible in traditionally male roles, and, perhaps, traditional beliefs in women's "uncleanness" have waned, making it easier to accept female *dang-gi*s. Even if this is true, a man or a woman who acts like Mrs. Tan did is extremely unlikely to be accepted as a *dang-gi* in Taiwan today.

Similarly, as will be detailed in the following chapter, Wolf's claims about the obliteration of women's name are exaggerated and overgeneralized to Taiwan, if they are valid in Hong Kong or anywhere else. At least during my lifetime, I do not think that Taiwanese sisters and daughters were as devalued as Western feminists, most influentially Margery Wolf, have maintained. My married(-out) sisters certainly remain very much a part of my family; daughters unquestionably are more highly valued in contemporary Taiwan than in representations of traditional China, including those that, beginning in the 1960s, were constructed from Taiwan as a place where that entity has been preserved through European and Japanese colonialisms and rapid socioeconomic "development."

## Intracultural Variation and Universal Explanations

In the final section of this chapter I want to supplement the response already made (in the notes) to the possible objections that I have substituted my assertions about an essentialized Taiwanese culture for Wolf's assertions about an essentialized Chinese culture or have minimized dissensus that can at least be glimpsed (though it is certainly not modeled) in Wolf 1992. While continuing in this section to deal with the particularities of the two cases contrasted earlier, what I am criticizing are common operating procedures in anthropology, not anything unique to Wolf's practices. In the process of setting herself up as arbiter of "ethnographic responsibility" (as an exemplar in invidious contrast to "postmodernists"), Wolf provided some rawer material (for Peihotieners, fieldnotes; for interpreting her own affect, a fictionalization of the events) than is usually the case for cooked cultural anthropological analyses (including mine) in which the ingredients of field observations have been carefully selected. *A Thrice Told Tale* is far from being the only example of imposing Western "scientific" explanations on alien religious behavior (see the critique in Ewing 1994). What Wolf wrote about Peihotien and her own procedures are used here as a synecdoche for anti-theistic and/or alien social science.

The material "Wu Chieh" gathered and that Wolf published three decades later contains evidence of initial uncertainty among villagers about how to understand Mrs. Tan's behavior. In particular, a 10 March 1960 note lists women aged sixty-four, fifty-seven, forty-three, and thirty-four and a man aged fifty-one as seeming to believe Mrs. Tan was a real *dang-gi*. It continues: "Most of the other women are still doubtful. During the afternoon events reported above, only 84 (M[ale] 39) and 330 (M 59) among the people in the crowd we talked with doubted that a god was somehow involved" (76). Earlier in the same entry (74) little boys saying, "This crazy lady is dancing," was noted. Despite her focus on gender, Wolf (1992) did not discuss a gender divide apparent in this note. The fieldnote lists thirty-four women and seven men who that day had been gathered around the house where Mrs. Tan was. This disparity suggests that fewer men than women thought the arrival of a god likely. Within even this biased sample most were doubtful. Four of thirty-four women and one of seven men seemed to believe; no women, two men, and some boys actively expressed disbelief. (It is unclear what the denominator of those "we talked with" is; one of the two men is not in the list of whom the crowd included on 71.) If the gendered distribution of interest could be clearly distinguished from the also gendered distribution of evaluation, intracultural variation (structured by gender) in each might be modeled. Rather than interpreting these data as showing different individual (or gender) models of what a *dang-gi* is or how to recognize one, I would interpret them as showing that the application of criteria are not always immediately obvious. There are two strong bases for this interpretation.

*Writing Based on Research on Taiwan*

The strongest is the very quick consensus that emerged a few days later. The other is that, even among those interested enough to hang about and see what Mrs. Tan would do next, there were four who were undecided for every one expressing even a tentative opinion for or against genuineness.

Other than being a woman, Li A-Koan is a prototypical instance of the Taiwanese category *dang-gi*, possessed by a deity particularly venerated in Taiwan and incarnated earlier in the same village. Not all Taiwanese believe in or go to *dang-gi*s for advice, and my family goes to a different *dang-gi*, but to the best of my knowledge no one from our natal village ever challenged Li A-Koan's legitimacy as a *dang-gi*.[30] Those who believe in the gods might accept a new god, but it is much more likely that the goddess we worship most and who has spoken before in our village will speak again than that a new one will appear. A new god has to prove himself (or, in the atheistic view, the *dang-gi* has to prove herself/himself). Since ghosts also possess people and try to pass themselves off as gods, new gods first have to convince people they are not ghosts. That the ghost question was raised about Mrs. Tan shows the normal working of Taiwanese criteria for sorting out unobvious cases of possible possession. In that most categories, especially social categories, are fuzzily bounded, one expects unanimity only about prototypical instances, not about cases at the edges.[31]

The heightened scrutiny of the non-prototypical instance focused on what Mrs. Tan did while possibly possessed by a new god. Villagers (and, later, outside experts) saw Mrs. Tan acting for herself (taking revenge on her enemies, attending to her children, and hauling her husband off for sex while supposedly possessed), not what would be expected if a god were possessing her (or, in the atheistic view, she displayed insufficient dissociation when supposedly in a trance). Had her possession not failed this test, the efficacy of what the god (or, in the atheistic view, she) recommended would have been evaluated, and there might have been a division between followers and non-followers, with some of the non-followers not believing she was possessed.

The case of Mrs. Tan does not seem to me evidence against the existence of an underlying shared model of what a genuine *dang-gi* is. How well an instance fits criteria for non-prototypical cases may be (and in this instance, for a time, was) debated, but this does not establish that there is not an agreed-upon cultural schema. I have argued that the checklist of features that Wolf presented are the wrong features (for emic or for etic analysis). There are some criterial features and a general consensus about what these are. There will be disagreement whether an instance fits a category if one or more criterial features are lacking in the instance. That some natives of a culture label an instance *A* and some not-*A* doesn't mean that there is not a category or schema, only that not every case can be easily classified. The two instances of extended concern here (Li A-Koan and Mrs. Tan), however, can be classified **and** were (first by Taiwanese villagers and also herein), one woman as "crazy," one woman as a genuine *dang-gi*.

My primary and secondary socialization on Taiwan and my ongoing conversations with other natives of Taiwan included inquiry into the questions "What is a *dang-gi*?" and "How can we recognize that a god is possessing someone?" In the considerable amount that she has published from it, there is no evidence that Margery Wolf's fieldwork involved systematic inquiry into these questions or that she sought to tap her field assistant's interpretation of Mrs. Tan or understanding of how other Taiwanese distinguish *dang-gis* from other kinds of persons. There is direct statement that neither religion nor healing was the primary focus of the fieldwork (102). A distrust of native explanations, common among anthropologists, that may rationalize an inability to secure or to understand them seems to me to be another reason for not asking more general questions about how to recognize a *dang-gi* or to explain why Mrs. Tan was not one, but such inferences about what is really going on are legitimate (apparently from the outraged reaction of anthropologist referees) only for anthropologists analyzing others, not when others are trying to make sense of why anthropologists do what they do.

In analyzing what project members wrote down from what "Wu Chieh" reported about what some villagers said about Mrs. Tan's behavior, Wolf seems to present herself as the careful, responsible analyst exemplifying that "much of a cultural onion may be as easily or even more easily picked apart by a careful analyst who is not of the culture" (5). In addition to questioning the care with which she considered data that "Wu Chieh" gathered that can be recovered from the 1960 fieldnotes, I reject the onion metaphor for either Taiwanese or Chinese culture. I would suggest, instead, that our culture is like one of a number of tropical fruits (mangosteen, durian, lichee). The alien anthropologist has peeled off the skin. Under the skin are not the same material in layer after layer, like an onion, but first pulp, then the fruit, then a membrane, then the generative core (seed). The kind of fieldwork that involves native assistants reporting some behaviors (in a lingua franca native to neither) seems to me not even to penetrate the skin and get to the pulp. Even if one gets to the pulp, one may still miss that there is a core, precisely the generative part. Research that does not even **seek** to learn what native generative models are and that substitutes explanation from the analytical categories aliens bring with them from what they are confident is a "superior" conceptual armory (here I mean scientific, not American) is almost certain to be unable to explain what some people decided or to predict future decisions.

What Wolf identified as the ethnographer's responsibility, "to get it right" (3), does not require turning anthropology over to natives (though training more "natives" to analyze their own cultures is a laudable endeavor) nor abandoning Western analytical concepts (though they could be used more carefully than Wolf did). To understand why Mrs. Tan was not accepted as a *dang-gi* requires analysis of Taiwanese plausibility criteria, **not** allegiance to them. In general "getting it right" requires seeking out and listening to native ideas and only substituting Western "scientific" ideas and categories with careful explanation of why such ideas more adequately account for observed (or observable) phenomena and why the natives are mistaken. As deployed by social scientists, explanatory concepts such as "class" and "gender" and "Chinese" explain too much too facilely.

# CHAPTER 9

# The Non-Obliteration of Taiwanese Women's Names

**M**argery Wolf (1990:429; 1992) claimed that the Taiwanese woman she calls Mrs. Tan in her "thrice told tale" of female victimization was "nameless, having lost her personal name at marriage," and invoked Watson (1986) as an authority on the loss of women's names in their shared reification of "Chinese culture" in the singular. Writing about rural Hong Kong, Watson (1986:626, 628) asserted that, at marriage,

> the bride enters a world in which she exists only in relation to others. She is no longer 'grounded' by her special [given] name (*ming*), however prosaic that name might have been; after marriage she exists only as someone's elder brother's wife or younger brother's wife or as Sing's mother, and so on. . . .
>
> Even in death a woman has no personal name. On the red flag that leads the spirit of the deceased from the village to the grave is written the woman's father's surname (for example Lin shih, translated "Family of Lin"); no personal name is added. . . . Neither do women's personal names appear on the tombstone where, again, only the surname of the woman's father is given ("Family of Lin").

Watson claimed that this pattern extends to "present-day rural Taiwan" (620),[1] but this is not so. In contemporary urban and rural Taiwan women retain their names. The household registries maintained by the police definitely include the women's names.[2] Growing up in Singong, a Holo (Hokkien)–speaking village in Daidiong County, I (KH) knew the name of my married women neighbors, and I certainly knew my mother's name. Moreover, her full name was used on the final public reference to her, her tombstone. So were my grandmothers'.

Although, like most Taiwanese, I go to cemeteries very reluctantly, pressed by Stephen Murray, who was eager to model variability in such final naming, I examined several hundred tombstones in a cemetery near

Sanxia in Daiba County, where Arthur and Margery Wolf did fieldwork. I could not find even one woman's grave that did not include her personal/given name. That is, there was no variance in the dependent variable to model.

With ever-mounting population pressure on even the steep hillsides of Taiwanese cemeteries, funeral plots are rented for only six to eight years at a time. Typically, and increasingly, one grave plot contains jars of the cleaned bones of multiple persons. Because bones are disinterred, cleaned, and reburied, the date of death of the (usually multiple) occupants of a gravesite is not generally recorded. Instead, the date of construction of the (often very elaborate) grave is carved on the stone. Names without dates are listed above the graves, the women's names being one character/surname longer. Although it is difficult to know what was inscribed when, there were some graves constructed during the 1950s, predating fieldwork by the Wolfs. I also asked a grave builder there if he knew of any women's graves with only reference to the woman's husband and sons. He did not, and he told me that he had recently replaced a more-than-200-year-old gravestone for a woman that included all her names.

Approximately eighty miles south, in the cemeteries of Bunchiuka, Singong, and Chientsui, where my ancestors are buried, I was able to find the graves of many women who died during the Qing Dynasty rule of the western Taiwan plains (that is, before 1895). Although many of the headstones had been erected more recently, it seems to me that, if the full name had not been on an earlier tombstone, it is unlikely to have been recalled and added to a later tombstone two or three generations later. That is, I assume names were copied. In the south of Taiwan (Jiaoshiong, Goyiong) I searched another cemetery for graves of women whose names were not preserved, and again I found none. My family may be especially bilateral (although I do not think it is; see Lu 2002:xiii; W.-P. Lin 2000), but, looking at the final reference/remembrance of many women, listing of their full names is routine from north to south on Taiwan.

This contrasts to the general American practice of listing only a married woman's personal name and her husband's name on tombstones. The form "née A," where A is the woman's patronym, is rare in contemporary American usages and was not used in twentieth-century "Anglo"-American tombstones I have seen. The Taiwanese style of listing husband's patronym and wife's patronym and given name is becoming more common in North America, with or without a hyphen between the two patronyms following the given/personal name. In Latin America sons have both father's and mother's patronyms (in yet another order). If the relation Watson envisioned between retention and/or number of names and women's status is valid (as I do **not** think it is), we would have to conclude that women's status is higher in Latin America than in Taiwan and higher in Taiwan (at least among the majority population) than in Anglo (white) North America.[3]

If Hong Kong and Taiwan both evidence that timeless and hardy essence "Chinese culture," I suspect that Watson (1986) did not take sufficient notice of distinctions between terms of address and terms of reference.[4] In the (uncited by Watson and Wolf) classic analysis of "Chinese terms of address" by Chao Yuen-Ren (1956)—who was known as "the father of Chinese linguistics" and who is surely the scholar with the broadest base for comparing usages among Chinese languages—is the statement "The sex of the speaker makes no great difference in terms of address, as it generally does not for other aspects of Chinese language" (240). While Chao (1956:240) acknowledged greater teknonymy **by** (not to) women, he noted that it was declining (in contrast to what Feng [1936] had reported). Chao (1956:223) also explicitly stated that "women have surnames, formal names, and courtesy names. . . . By the time a girl is old enough to use a courtesy name, she often gets married and is then socially known as Mrs. So-and-so." The last is considered by many "natives" to be a courtesy name.

Obviously, tombstones refer to rather than address a person. I would not deny that we use first, second, third, and so on, "sister-in-law" in address (not *N*th "brother's wife," as many Westerners suppose). However, paralleling, and perhaps influenced by, Japanese models (see T. Suzuki 1978:106), we use given names for **younger** brothers' wives. That is, their husbands' relative birth order determines whether a sister-in-law is addressed with her personal name or with what we conceive to be the **more deferential** "first [or *N*th] sister-in-law." This pattern would appear to be traditional in Beijinghua (Mandarin) as well, since Chao (1956:236–37) included these rules:

> In speaking to a superior, reference to his relative should always be made in terms of the speaker's relationship.
>
> From equal-younger-down one begins to speak of one's relatives by name.
>
> Speaking to an inferior is very simple. One does not address him by terms of relationship, but by name.

It bears stressing that, in Chao's model for "Chinese," relative status as well as relative age are important in generating output (for address or for reference). Sex is not.

In Taiwan, and probably across the range of Sino-Tibetan languages, outside the family it is proper to address a woman as "Mrs. B," where *B* is her husband's name, as it has been in Anglo North America and remains so in much of it. Similarly, "Penelope's mom" is not an unusual term of reference but is very unusual beyond the first meeting as a term of address. "Oh, hi! So you're Penny's mom" is appropriate for an adult who knows the child Penelope Rice and is encountering the Penelope's mother for the first time. Prototypically, this would be followed by "I'm C." If *C* is a first name, the next turn is likely to be a return of a first name as a self-identification, whereas "I'm Mrs. C" is likely to lead to "I'm Mrs. Rice," and "I'm John Taylor's wife" is likely to lead to "I'm Jerry Rice's wife," with subsequent symmetrical address by either first name or by *Mrs.* plus the husband's name.[5]

Taiwanese men's names are replaced in address and in reference by their positions in the family or other role structures more than North American Anglo men's are, choice being primarily governed by their status relative to the speaker. To both men **and** women we use title–plus–family name ("Mr. B" and "Mrs. B") far more frequently than do Anglo North Americans. Given greater sexual segregation in Taiwan than in North America, the intimate exchanging of personal names between men and women is quite rare in Taiwan. The power differential of titling upward and personal naming downward that Brown and Gilman (1960) and their many followers have found is not structured by gender in Taiwan, although the asymmetric pattern is structured by other statuses there.

Until very recently, Western scholarship about Taiwan has overestimated the extent to which a married woman is lost to her natal family.[6] In recent years, when I have been able to visit Taiwan (after being blacklisted and refused entry for more than two decades), I have stayed at the house of one of my married sisters (whom I always address with her given name), probably not coincidentally the one who carried me around on her back when I was an infant (*aigua e duazi*). Not only my other married sister and her husband, but also the family of the deceased sister who lived to adulthood have visited me and provided hospitality. Indeed, I have been chauffeured by sons of two of my three sisters and by none of the sons of my six brothers (though they have given me bus directions and sometimes accompanied me to the right bus stop). Schak (1991) showed that, although aid is more likely to be supplied by agnatic kin, affines are significantly often the source of help for poor Taiwanese. By his reckoning sisters supplied 70 percent as much aid as brothers, and persons in the matriline 80 percent as much as those in the patriline. He and Stafford (1992:371) suggested that Taiwanese women evidence considerable filial piety. As early as a generation earlier, Chen (1977) had already noted that the duties of worshipping their husband's ancestors were being taken over by wives in rural Taiwan.

With the continued marked reduction in family size on Taiwan in recent decades, an array of male descendants is increasingly rare, boosting parents' dependence on daughters for future support (both in old age and after death). Daughters are also increasingly **able** to provide support. As married women increasingly remain employed (see Lee 1998; Yi and Chien 2001), we can anticipate further rises in Taiwanese men's valuation of daughters. In a Bindong fishing village where he did fieldwork Stafford (1992:374–75) reported: "Many of the grandparents I knew were as interested in the children of their daughters as of their sons, and more than one person told me they thought it was best to forget tradition and be happy with daughters, who were less trouble than unmanageable boys." The contemporary view is that daughters provide earlier, more reliable, and often as substantial returns on the investment in raising them in comparison to sons (also see Tu et al. 1992; and, for fertility-curtailed China, Gong 2002). I know that my father accompanied my second sister's son when he took his senior high school entrance exam, showing that, even with seven sons, he considered his married daughters and their offspring still to be a significant part of our family.

Another indication that women's status has been higher in traditional Taiwanese than in traditional Chinese culture is that in Taiwanese opera women play some of the leading male parts, while in "Peking opera" men played all the parts.

Although lacking in officially legitimated authority, wives and mothers have long exercised considerable power on Taiwanese men, as no one has shown more clearly than Margery Wolf (1968, 1972). It is ironic that someone who popularized the view of the powerful maternal bonds of the "uterine family" beneath the veneer of male (Confucian) ideology, and who has made individual Taiwanese women (including "the woman who didn't become a shaman" and her mother) vivid to Western readers, should contend that Taiwanese women's identities are indistinct early on and then totally obliterated by marriage.

More generally, Spiro (1993:121–22) warned against confusing designation—even "self-presentation"—with "self-representation" and, specifically, against inferring from the existence or even the use of titles rather than personal names that those so designated fail to perceive themselves as "unique creatures with a private fate." That women's selves are not so easily obliterated by confinement to "dependency relationships" was shown by those such as el-Messeri (1978), Ewing (1990), and Wikan (1980, 1990), who studied women's lives rather than taking male ideology as an adequate account of the de facto status of women in ideologically very patriarchal Islamic societies. Weller (1999:25) argues that "a firm sense of self was central to the [Confucian] philosophy." The Buddhist doctrine that the self is an illusion (*anatta*) failed to be accepted and internalized in China and the West Pacific or even in the officially Buddhist states of Southeast Asia (Elvin 1985:170; Spiro 1993:119–20). Taiwanese are less doctrinaire Buddhists than Indochinese or Chinese Buddhists. Indeed, as discussed earlier in this volume, Taiwanese are exceptionally pluralistic in deity picking.

## Conclusions

The claims by Watson and Wolf about the obliteration of women's name are exaggerated and overgeneralized to Taiwan, if they are or were valid in Hong Kong or anywhere else. At least during my lifetime (which reaches back a decade before American anthropologists arrived there) I do not think that Taiwanese sisters and daughters were as devalued as Western feminists have maintained. Although the use of personal names as an indicator of status is not valid, American anthropologists have been wrong about both the facts and interpretations of the obliteration of Taiwanese women's personal names.

Daughters unquestionably are more highly valued in contemporary Taiwan than in representations of "traditional China," including those that, beginning in the 1960s, constructed Taiwan as a place where that entity has been preserved through European and Japanese colonialism and through recent rapid socioeconomic "development."

# CHAPTER 10

## The Aftermath: Fleeing Democratization

To me (KH), as to many Taiwanese, it seems that American anthropologists are afraid of democracy and believe that they must depend on authoritarian states to force people to be studied by ignorant aliens speaking (if usually awkwardly) the language imposed by that state. When opposition to the KMT was not permitted and the KMT ruled Taiwan under martial law, American anthropologists were abundantly present—writing about "Chinese culture," using Beijinghua as a lingua franca to villagers whose mother tongue was Holo or Hakka and who had been schooled in Japanese. Then, when those who had been schooled in Beijinghua started to grow up and the KMT began including Taiwanese at higher levels in the party and democratization began to follow Taiwanization and increased prosperity, almost all of the American anthropologists fled. Seemingly, they were not interested in observing democratization and/or were not comfortable when the ROC government could not so easily impose foreign social scientists on Taiwanese and stopped pressing claims to Chineseness and to constituting the rightful government of China (thereby having less interest in anthropologists calling what they observed "Chinese culture").

Most of the anthropologists who were interested in doing fieldwork fled democratizing Taiwan for China, where the authoritarian government was still able—and now was more willing—to impose foreign social researchers on its people. I know that motivation is more complicated than fearing democracy and seeking the protection of authoritarian sponsorship, though these elements seem at least to be **involved**. Those who had been looking through Taiwanese people, culture, and society to write about "Chinese" this or that had not wanted to work on Taiwan or to pay attention to Taiwanese people except as surrogates for unavailable Chinese. China is what interested them, where they wanted to but could not go.

Coeditor of *The Anthropology of Taiwanese Society* Hill Gates (1999:1) wrote candidly, "In the 1960s, the United States forbade its citizens to visit China, and neither side was prepared to have social investigators living there. Instead, I did fieldwork in Taiwan." When it became possible to work in the PRC, "after two decades of depression, my energy was back, and I was ravenous to begin the China anthropology that had so long eluded me" (2). Her book about her "adventures in China" discussed how Chinese women in Sichuan were forced to cooperate with her research. Gates had the grace to be uncomfortable with the element of coercion that procured her "informants" and data. She was also candid that the academic rewards for research on China are higher than those for research on Taiwan (though she underestimates the importance of this by labeling it "academic snobbery") in a 1988 journal entry:

> No matter what superficialities I return with from Chengdu, they will count for something simply because they come from China, and not Taiwan. I am going to obtain data by what are primarily fetch-me-a-pygmy [that is, coerced informants], yet I am already [at the start of her fieldwork in Sichuan] receiving invitations from real universities to lecture on this perhaps too-quick research. More fuss will doubtless be made about my four months here than has ever been over the four years of sweat, tears, and lowered serotonin levels that the Taiwan findings have cost me. (In Gates 1999:68–69)

The theorists little inclined to fieldwork continue to (over)generalize from written materials and bits of their earlier thin ethnography to "Chinese" culture. The anthropology of religion using Taiwanese data continues to be a domain in which data from Taiwan has been most insistently forced into the Chinese rubric. This has continued to be the case in books heavy with theorizing, such as Feuchtwang (1992) and Sangren (1987).

Arthur Wolf, another anthropologist whose work shows a preference for poring over records extracted by plantation-like neocolonial labor (see Chun 2000:589), rather than doing ethnography, produced his magnum opus on childhood association's de-eroticizing daughters-in-law adopted as children. As in his earlier work, its primary basis on Taiwanese evidence was occluded from the book's title (*Sexual Attraction and Childhood Association: A **Chinese** Brief for Edward Westermarck*).

Hill Gates (1997, 1999), Melissa Brown (1996), and Robert Weller (1986, 1994) explicitly compare material from Taiwan and material from China. Perhaps from having become accustomed to peripherality (and little competition from other anthropologists?), American anthropology professors who have shifted their fieldwork from Taiwan to China have mostly chosen to work not in the central plains, which are the heartland of "traditional Han Chinese culture" and the basis for the appellation "Middle Kingdom." Instead, they have gone to Han peripheries (for example, Hill Gates, David Schack) or on non-Han peoples within the PRC (for example, Burton Pasternak and Stevan Harrell). Evidence of the continued heedlessness by anthropologists to complicity with domination is the pathetically circumscribed scope of "fieldworkers' responsibilities in China" posited by Pasternak (1983:61–62): he does not consider anything problematic about contributing to the legitimacy of ethnic (or any other kind of) domination and systematic state ethnocide but addressed the need to give lectures while in the field in China.

Social scientists, mostly Taiwanese sociologists, who have published on an increasingly democratic Taiwan in which even the Kuomintang was Taiwanized have empirically examined the previously taboo topic of ethnic identity and cultural differences on the multiethnic island,[1] even if the source of the data being Taiwan is sometimes still occluded by Western anthropologists (for example, Stafford 1995). A 2000 special issue of the *International Journal of the Sociology of Language* included scrutiny of language use and Taiwanese identity by Huang Shuanfan, Liao Chao-Chih, and John Kwock-Ping Tse (also see Sandel 2003). Identity politics and party (re)alignment has been analyzed by Kim (2000a, b), Lu (2002), You (1994), and Wu Nai-Teh (1992, 2002).

Gender, the dominant discourse within American anthropology during the most recent two decades (see Murray 1994), has been a major focus of anthropological research done on Taiwan (see Moskowitz 2001; Wen 2000). The presence of women in the paid labor force has remained the primary interest, but, rather than the unmarried temporary factory workers living in dormitories described by Diamond (1979) and Kung (1984), the later research focused on women doing piecework at home (Hsiung 1996; Lee 2000) or those who are capitalist entrepreneurs (Gates 1997; Y. Lu 2001; Simon 2000, 2003b; Wilen 1995) has fired ethnographers' interest recently. Diverse patterns of continued employment for women after marriage and giving birth were elucidated by sociologists Yi and Chien (2001) and Yu (2001), while Chang Chin-Fen (2002) found systematic discrimination against female workers in state-owned enterprises as well as in private companies.

## One Partial Exception to the Pattern of Flight from Democracy

Robert P. Weller's book *Alternate Civilities: Democracy and Culture in China and Taiwan* (1999) attends to the recent sociopolitical history of Taiwan, in particular to the florescence since the lifting of martial law of "civil society," that is, the growth of "intermediate" institutions not sponsored by the state or by families (see Schatz 2000; Warren 2000). Weller argues that post–martial law Taiwan shows that a Chinese cultural tradition does not preclude democracy, challenging the claims not only of the Chinese Communist Party but of Singapore's former prime minister Lee Kuan-Yew, who has long justified repressive paternalism in Singapore on the basis of a dependent character and essentialized Chinese culture that requires authoritarian rule.

Nevertheless, Weller's project is still to look through Taiwan to see China. The novelty is that it is a future democratic China he is looking for rather than a pickled Ming Dynasty Chinese culture preserved and available for study by Western scholars. Still, Weller does explicitly examine Taiwanese materials (religious associations, business associations, and environmentalist groups) and keeps clear what data come from Taiwan, what from China. He marshals evidence of a rapid growth in civil society in Taiwan since the lifting of martial law and of a (much slower) growth of civil society in the PRC since the end of the Great Proletarian Cultural Revolution.[2] Following the collapse of the Soviet Empire, it has become clear that "totalitarian régimes" are not as monolithic as was supposed during the 1950s. That is, they did not have total control enabling them to annihilate completely all associations and institutions intermediate between the individual and the state (the PRC and its ally the Khmer Rouge tried the hardest; the KMT was not a slacker in this regard either). Weller points to parallels between the kinds of local ties and organizations that exist in China now and those that existed under KMT martial law. In both instances great care has/had to be taken to claim such associations were not political.

Although much of his own research has been on the covert resistance to the state, particularly as expressed in popular religion, Weller may not realize the extent to which protests against polluters was a way of challenging the KMT regime—not just state-owned and party-owned industries (including the Taiwan Power Company, which owns the nuclear power plants) but companies of KMT cronies and supporters. Protesting pollution was a wedge to challenge the way the government exploited the island (see Kim 2000; M. Ho 2001). This was especially the case in the interim years between the lifting of martial law and the end of sedition laws used to quash criticism of the KMT regime.

Protests could be legitimated with the Confucian value of saving resources for *zisun* (descendants), as Weller (1999:118) recognizes, though he goes astray, interpreting invocation of preserving the earth for *zisun* as meaning preserving it for the male line. There may be a contrast in rhetoric between predominantly female environmental organizations and primarily male ones, but the difference is one of time depth—the contrast being of the children already born rather than generations yet to be born—but the distinction is **not** between offspring of both sexes and sons. Weller does not provide any evidence that Taiwanese understand *zisun* in the narrow sense of his interpretation (as male offspring only). The English word *patrimony* (which Weller uses and which does not contrast to *matrimony*) is etymologically unilateral but in contemporary usage (in societies with bilateral inheritance) is often understood to mean what parents of both sexes give or preserve for their children of both sexes, not what fathers give or preserve for their sons. Attributing a male line–only reading that strikes me as latter-day Orientalist exaggeration of difference(s).

Weller claimed that, "by comparing China with the vibrant democracy that has developed over the last decade in Taiwan, I show how civil society can grow out of Chinese cultural roots and authoritarian institutions" (1999:xii). He is not so rash as to argue that a vibrant civil society and democracy **will** blossom in China: Weller does not suggest democratization is inevitable, cautioning that "social organizations do not automatically lead to democratization and that corporatist arrangements like the one Taiwan had [under KMT martial law] can go on for decades" (1999:143). Recent Taiwanese social history shows that the often-invoked essential need for authoritarian rule has been disconfirmed. His challenge to a deterministic "culture of authoritarianism" is salutary, but it seems to me that predictions based on the analogy of Taiwan to China need to consider not only the differences in scale but also the far greater influence of an American democratic ethos on the current generation of leaders in Taiwan. Most of those who constitute the current DPP government of Taiwan were, earlier in their lives, students in the United States. There have also been many students in U.S. universities from the PRC, but, whereas many of the Taiwanese students protested KMT rule from the safety of the United States, students from China criticizing communist rule is a null set (excepting those who fled immediately after the Tiananmen massacre and sought permanent asylum in the United States). Moreover, very few of the current rulers of China have lived abroad and observed more open and democratic societies on more than brief official visits.

Although we certainly hope that Weller is right about the likely telos of history, what is relevant here is that he provides another example of failing to register the extent of non-Chinese influence on contemporary Taiwanese lives and worldviews. Although he stresses the need to root understanding of "Taiwan's democratic transition in its specific social and historical context" (1999:143), he seems to underplay Japanese and American **cultural** influences and even the extent of **economic** investments that first the Japanese (as Taiwan's colonial master) and then the United States (under the guise of shoring up a bulwark against communism) made. These investments in infrastructure—including human infrastructure through education—are very important to the success in the world market that Taiwanese enterprises had in the 1980s and 1990s. (Weller is very mindful that the florescence of intermediate institutions was financed by the resulting prosperity.)

## Conclusion

Some Anglophone anthropologists writing about Taiwan, such as Charles Stafford, continue to seek the greater prestige of studying Chinese culture with titles (and discourses) that obscure the site of their fieldwork. Most of the American anthropologists who did fieldwork on Taiwan when China was closed to them moved on to their real interest when the post-Mao communist regime allowed foreigners greater access to China. Some (for example, Sangren, Arthur and Margery Wolf) have continued to draw on material gathered earlier on Taiwan while continuing to package what they write as being about Chinese phenomena. A few, such as Weller and Gates, are interested in contrasting lifeways and associations in Taiwan to those in China, though mostly seeming to regard Taiwanese phenomena as possible harbingers of the future for China (rather than as remnants of Ming Dynasty China, as in much of the anthropological writing based on materials from Taiwan during the 1950s and 1960s).

We do not mean to suggest that the published descriptions of Taiwanese communities are without value, though their usefulness as history of the KMT era is reduced by a general reluctance to describe state terrorism by the regime that permitted anthropologists to do fieldwork in Taiwan and the mystification of identity and language of those studied. The price of admission to do fieldwork on Taiwan during the KMT era seems to have included obscuring power relations and paralleling the Chiang dictatorship's portrayal of Taiwan as a Chinese culture, though in most conventional senses Taiwan was more "modern" than China was when Chiang was driven out of China and took refuge on Taiwan. Despite a turn to reflexivity in recent American anthropology, there has been a notable lack of reflection on the ideological service anthropologists have provided either to the right-wing Leninist ROC regime or to the left-wing Leninist PRC one.

# Acknowledgments

We are grateful for some support in the form of an Ong Iotek Award from the Taiwan Foundation for formulation of the analysis of *dang-gis* and for bibliographic assistance from Pong Wenshen. Earlier versions of portions of this book were presented at annual meetings of the American Anthropological Association, the American Sociological Association, the North American Taiwan Studies Association, and the North American Taiwanese Professors' Association. We would like to acknowledge the encouragement and comments by the audiences as well as those by Roberto Alvarez, Fredrik Barth, Jonathan Benthall, Russell Bernard, Judith Farquhar, Carol Brooks Gardner, Hill Gates, Timothy Halkowski, Jane Hill, Claude Lévi-Strauss, Lo Mingchen, Robert M. Marsh, Ng Mi-Yen, Donald Nonini, Shu Wei-Der, Richard Stamps, William Tang, David Tsai, Unni Wikan, Wang Yichun, and George Yeh on drafts of earlier portions of this book and by Regna Darnell, Gary Dunham, and Li Khîn-Hoâ on the entire book. The authors bear sole responsibility for the book's contents.

An earlier version of chapter 7 was published in *Dialectical Anthropology* 16 (© 1992 by Kluwer Academic Publishing). Earlier drafts of some other material appeared in *Anthropology Today*, *Typhoon* (the newsletter of the Taiwan Forum of the University of California, Berkeley), the *Taiwan Tribune*, the *Northern California Formosan Federation Newsletter*, as a working paper of El Instituto Obregón, and in our 1994 book, *Taiwanese Culture, Taiwanese Society*, which is primarily an annotated bibliography of American anthropology and sociology publications on the topic through 1992.

Although Margery Wolf did not reply to a request, made (accompanied by a stamped and pre-addressed reply envelope) shortly after the publication of her paper in the *American Ethnologist*, for the three characters she romanized as "Shang Ti Kung" (the deity the unhappy Taiwanese woman claimed to be possessed by), if it were not for Wolf and the many anthropologists eager to ward off any discussion of the adequacy of analysis even by someone such as Wolf with no professional training, no command of the language spoken by the people being analyzed, no command of the basic technical distinctions, and no respect for the beliefs she claimed to analyze, this book would not exist.

Continuing to try to understand Wolf's opaque romanizations, I sought the aid of the editor of the *American Ethnologist* to get clarification of one name and one other word from an unspecified Sino-Tibetan language in her article. That request was similarly ignored. Without making any charges of any sort, I also wrote the ethics committee of the American Anthropological Association (the umbrella organization that includes the American Ethnological Society, publisher of the *American Ethnologist*) asking about standards for requests from natives for clarifications very limited in scope about materials published in AAA journals. This query, too, went unanswered.

Wolf expanded her article into a book (1992) that has been widely used in women's studies courses. One of the topics listed in its subtitle was "ethnographic responsibility." From my own experience I knew that she did not consider this to include specifying native terms inscribed in her texts, even when a native asked to know what they were, another instance of what Chun (2000:589) characterizes as "hacienda" anthropology in regard to another Wolf enterprise. From the book I also learned that she does not see anything wrong with publishing work by others (in this case a research assistant) without including their names. Her decision to obliterate the name of the Taiwanese woman who wrote the second of the three renditions of the tale of the woman who did not become (recognized as) a *dang-gi* is especially ironic given that a major—though mistaken—part of Wolf's (1990, 1992) argument is that Taiwanese women's names are obliterated.

The KMT finally lifted martial law on Taiwan in 1987 and abolished the blacklist in 1992. Dissidents like me, previously classified as "terrorists," were able to revisit Taiwan. I was thus able to supplement my memories of growing up there. As I discussed in chapter 8, I had thought that a woman could not be a *dang-gi*, but, when I returned, one lived literally across the road from my childhood home. I submitted an article contrasting the two instances to the *American Ethnologist*. A referee for the journal complained that the title—"A Taiwanese Woman Who Became a Shaman," dropping one word from the title of Wolf's article—was "a personal attack." This shows the extraordinary extension of "personal attack" seemingly rampant in contemporary anthropology. American Anthropological Association annual meeting organizers—specifically referring to Derek Freeman's critique of Margaret Mead's claims about Samoa—admitted that they wanted to avoid the spectacle of another American woman anthropologist being criticized for ethnographic incompetence and theoretical bias by a non-American(-born) man.

I thought that I had made rather modest claims to the authority of a native, in that I had begun the paper (as in chap. 8 here) by discussing my own misplaced belief that a woman could not be a *dang-gi*. By starting with this example of native **fallibility**, I had tried to make clear that I did not think that natives qua natives are always right and alien observers invariably wrong. Given the violent reaction and highly motivated misreading of what I wrote, I cannot help thinking that writing in the first-person singular, as a Taiwanese, rather than in the distanced third person scared reviewers who were insecure about their own shaky authority as outsiders with limited competence or no competence in the mother tongue of the majority of the populations they wrote about. Another referee suggested that I should sympathize with the handicaps native speakers of English have doing field-work in Taiwan (without providing any charity to me as an author writing in what is, chronologically, my fourth language). The most interesting reviewer comment resurrected (presumably from his or her student days) Lévi-Strauss's blanket rejection of any native model as being necessarily obscurantist, accusing me of "being blinded by indigenous categories," of producing "reverse Orientalism,"[1] and of being "biased against using materials from other Chinese cultural settings to interpret Taiwanese findings." I had argued, as in chapter 9 here, that, even if the pattern was true for Hong Kong, it was not true for Taiwan and that findings from Hong Kong cannot simply be extrapolated to Taiwan. And, far from blanket rejection of any analysis of any Chinese phenomena having relevance for patterning on Taiwan, I used Chao Yuen-Ren's classic analysis (conveniently published in English in 1956) of Beijing usage to show that gender is not a major determinant of Chinese address or reference (either).

Not all assertions, and still less interpretations built on them, are as easily settled as is that of the inclusion of women's names on their final resting places. The obscurantist fog of postmodernist writing (the pervasiveness of which Wolf also deplores) keeps the alien "professional" in charge of orchestrating the voices permitted within discourse about "others" and avoids holding them accountable for selection of data and interpretations even more thoroughly than what postmodernists dismiss as "naive empiricism." Anthropology's gatekeepers seem to view me either as a simple-minded/old-fashioned scientist who has not heard that all interpretations are arbitrary or as someone deluded by indigenous categories and models.

Someone like me who knows my culture from inside and is fluent in its two most-used languages could not possibly understand the (un- or mis-specified) value of their models and the often opaque representations of sagacious "specialists." They are determined to keep deciding what is interesting about any culture or society and whether insights from those not properly initiated into the mysteries of representation theories should be used to make statements about villages, industrializing nations, China, humankind, and perhaps even Taiwan—the level of analysis that has been unthinkable to Margery and Arthur Wolf and to most of the other American anthropologists who made their careers by mining social and cultural materials on Taiwan before getting to the Big Leagues—or at least the behemoth that is the PRC.

# Notes

## 1. A "Native" Observing Anthropology

1. This is even more true of Chinese anthropologists working in Taiwan than of Westerners. Taiwanese anthropologists are in quasi-feudal dependence and lack autonomy in choosing research topics (see Chun 2000b). The warrant (to follow American examples) for treating rural Taiwan as a space in which to examine Chinese culture and society was supplied by Chen Shao-Hsing 1966.

2. Hong and Murray 1989; Murray and Hong 1988, 1991, 1994; Hong 1994.

3. However unskeptical about its claims, most of the "political science" writing about Taiwan has noted that the KMT/ROC regime was not ruling China, that is, that the governments of Taiwan and China were not the same. Similarly, economists have shown themselves able to distinguish Taiwanese from Chinese economies and economic arrangements.

4. For example, Harrell and Huang (1994:13), in what they attribute to Murray and Hong 1988, ignoring the response to Harrell that was Hong and Murray 1989. One would have to believe that Harrell never saw his own publication in the core journal of the American Anthropological Association to claim that he could have been unaware of the response beginning on the same page.

5. Perry Anderson (2004) noted that the earliest modern form of nationalism, preceding the German romantic notions of *Völkgeist*, was "the separation of overseas settler communities from an imperial homeland." This sort of national identity required no major linguistic or ethnic difference from the metropolis; rather, "markers of nascent national identity were territorial and historical: Geographical distance and colonial institutions engendered a distinct culture and self-consciousness and therewith a collective identity that laid the foundation for independent states." He stressed (taking the American Revolution as a prime example) that "a political—as distinct from linguistic, ethnic, or cultural—construction of the nation is not unusual in the history of settler nationalisms."

## 2. The Investigation of "Others" before 1955

1. Eric Wolf (1969) discussed the role of post-peasants in the czarist army and the ultimate success of the Bolshevik revolution in the countryside (though state

power was seized, initially, by St. Petersburg workers). The long-running Mexican Revolution also had a substantial component of peasant uprising and institution-alized a government that expropriated American oil companies during the 1930s.

### 3. The History of Governing Taiwan

1. Lamley (1981) showed that cooperation (and intermixture) marked the pioneering stage of Chinese settlements on Taiwan. Holo-Hakka discord increased during the last half-century of Qing rule. Concerted efforts to readopt customs and practices—especially religious observations—native to their place of origin were key markers of difference. Religion continued to be a vehicle for expressing (through masks transparent to everyone) opposition to Japanese and KMT rule (see Gates 1981; Weller 1987) and, after dissent began to be allowed, ceased to be treated as sedition (see Katz 2003).

2. Chuang (1988) expands upon the thesis of the independence of Taiwanese economic development from Qing policy.

3. Taiwanese were excluded from government posts. These were reserved first for Japanese and then Chinese colonial masters. Medicine was one field in which Taiwanese could attain professional status (see Lo 2001). Limited educational opportunities induced very disproportionately greater numbers of ethnic Taiwanese to opt for running their own business as the path to upward mobility in contrast to Mainlanders with the sinecures of the "iron rice bowl" (*tie fan wan*, that is, state-sector jobs); see H-Z Wang 2001, 2002.

4. All quotations are from the English-language text of the treaty and from the verbatim "Record of Proceedings/Conference for the Conclusion and Signature of the Treaty of Peace with Japan" published in 1951 by the U.S. State Department. That this provision was 2.b stimulates curiosity about what 2.a was. Provision 2.a is parallel in renouncing territory long occupied by Japan on the Korean peninsula and in not stipulating to what government it was surrendering "all right, title, and claim."

### 4. A Case Study of Pseudo-Objectivity

1. Both KMT apologists such as Lai et al. and KMT opponents use the date 28 February 1947 to stand in for the events of the following weeks or years. *Incident* is a reasonable locution for the attack on a Taiwanese woman selling contraband cigarettes and the immediate counterattack of bystanders, but the troops sent by Chiang Kai-Shek from China did not arrive shooting until 8 March. The chapter in George Kerr's (1965) *Formosa Betrayed* about the start of the reign of terror is titled "The March Massacre," and in the book's dedication Kerr wrote that

> by March 17 the pattern of terror and revenge had emerged very clearly.
> First to be destroyed were all established critics of the Government. Then in their turn came Settlement Committee members and their principal aides, all youths who had taken part in the interim policing of Taipei, middle school students, middle school teachers, lawyers, economic leaders and members of

influential families, and at last, anyone who had in the preceding eighteen months had given offense to a mainland Chinese, causing him to "lose face." On March 16, it was reported that anyone who spoke English reasonably well, or who had close foreign connections, was being seized for "examination." (1965:299–300)

2. Such extreme identification with KMT misrule continues in American social science discourse—for example, Wachman's (1995:92) egregiously biased explanation of "the friction between the KMT and Taiwanese stemming from persistent memories of initial misperceptions and early conflicts . . . a legacy of frustration resulting from the authoritarian nature of KMT rule, which seemed [!] to favor Mainlanders and their interests over the Taiwanese, and which, in an effort to resocialize Taiwanese as Chinese, inadvertently reinforced mutual perceptions of difference."

3. It is difficult not to see such blaming the press for fomenting dissatisfaction through lack of respect of the government in the right-wing American discourse, particularly in a book coming from the Hoover Institution, a place that it is hard to conceive of as a home of political neutrality.

4. Given the KMT/Hoover Institution view that Taiwan is intrinsically a part of China, it is curious that Ch'en Yi's Chinese subordinates had "less understanding of local conditions" (87) than Japanese colonialists had had.

5. They plausibly argued (176–77) that Ch'en Yi did not want to have to request the diversion of troops from the mainland civil war. However, this does not make clear at what point he began to buy time with concessions he did not intend to honor while planning later repression. The authors were quick to credit Ch'en Yi with "sincerity" in this—as in other matters—although it seems very unlikely that Ch'en ever meant to share power or clean up the rampant corruption of his government.

6. A rare exception to the lack of agents is "Gen. P'eng Meng-Chi, commander of the Kaohsiung [Go'hiong] Fortress HQ . . . ordered the massacres in Kaohsiung and Tainan" (161).

### 6. Studies of KMT-Imposed Land Reform

1. For instance, 38 percent of former tenants built new houses, 39 percent repaired houses, and 61 percent of current tenants rebuilt or repaired their houses. Not knowing how many former tenants both repaired and built houses, it is not even clear which group did more home improvement. Depending on how many former tenants both repaired and built houses, 61 percent compares to some percentage between 39 and 77.

2. H.-H. Chen (1975:378–79) challenged the contention that small farms are less efficient by showing that the value of output per hectare of farms of less than a half-hectare was NT$40,900, in contrast to NT$26,700 for larger farms. The output per man was $20,000, however, was in contrast to $25,000 for larger farms. C.-

L. Hwang (1968) reported that 1963 yields per family for tenant farmers was NT$29,877, in contrast to $34,653 for owners, and $39,095 for part owners. These data suggest that owners produce more than tenants and part owners/part tenants produce still more (per person rates were $30,000, $40,000, $43,000, respectively).

3. However, the same authors (Kuo et al. 1981:50) later wrote that "land reform was the primary ingredient of sustained increase of agricultural productivity in the early 1950s."

### 7. Looking through Taiwan to See China

1. See the bibliography in Passin 1947. For an overview of work published in Chinese, see *Symposium on Taiwan Aborigines: Retrospect and Prospect* (*Bulletin of the Institute of Ethnology, Academia Sinica* 40 [1975]).

2. Pressures and cultural expectations for early family division are a central concern in Margery Wolf's (1972) *Women and the Family in Rural Taiwan*. In contrast, another pioneer American ethnographer of rural Taiwan, Bernard Gallin, explicitly distinguished Taiwanese and Chinese practices in the first American ethnography of a Taiwanese village, *Hsin Hsing, Taiwan*.

3. Although few anthropologists today are as determined to sort out the sources of cultural traits as Boasians and diffusionists were in the first third of the twentieth century, there is still an equation of *genuine* with *original*, a distaste for historical complexity, and a continuing quest for at least relative "purity" of "tradition." See Fichte 1985:285; Murray 1981, 1999.

4. The sense of some Taiwanese that their religion is related to Hinduism and the borrowing and transformation of Hindu deities might stimulate research to investigate a "folk brahman complex" carried with Buddhism, as in its diffusion to Thailand; see Kirsch 1977: 252; and Tambiah 1970.

5. For a very Durkheimian view of the primacy of social accommodation over imaginable doctrinal conflicts, see Reischauer 1981:138–45; also see Smith 1983:16, 29, 110–14.

6. Similarly, in using Japanese colonial records, Barrett (1990) attributed a similarity between colonial Japanese and Taiwanese seasonality of birth to climate rather than to culture, without considering the possible importance of Japanese culture in an article the title of which purports that it is about "traditional Chinese."

7. In the same preface (x) Wolf mentioned that data from land title registers and land tax registers was being culled to collate with the household registry data, so perhaps *yet* should be added, even nearly two decades after he wrote this statement. Given the frequency of land transactions, the noncontiguity of holdings, and the variations in grade of land, estimating the value or yield of property owned by families in Japanese Taiwan is not at all an easy task.

8. One cannot extrapolate directly from these discrepancies to the Japanese period. Although the KMT took over the institution of household registration and increased police surveillance, short-term and long-term migration to Daiba and to other cities was clearly higher than in the Japanese era, providing an increased

118           

opportunity for registering family members who were living in other places than where they were officially counted.

9. In the view of the Qing official who gladly arranged to give the island to the Japanese, Li Hongzhang (Li Hung Chang 1913), the nonaboriginal Taiwanese were even more degraded than the aboriginal "wild beasts" head-hunting in the hills. In reporting the Mainlander derogation of Taiwanese, I do not intend to denigrate the aboriginal population, and (obviously) do not accept the equation of *Chinese* with *superior*.

10. I consider insider views of Taiwanese religion in "A Taiwanese Woman Who Became a Spirit Medium" (chap. 8). Here I am dealing only with external "rational" explanations of religious phenomena.

11. A resurgence of long-suppressed popular religion (along with a renaissance of elaborate funerals) also emerged as part of southern resistance to the northern and iconoclastic communist regime in China; see Luo 1991; and Friedman 1993.

12. An excellent example of more recently fashionable social construction of "tradition" analysis was provided by Handler (1988). For cautions that "authenticity is not a function of antiquity and recency is not evidence of triviality" in cultural patterning, see Smith 1989:722. Native concerns with such analyses were sensitively considered by Jackson 1989.

13. A concise account is contained in Grayson 1979:34–47.

14. Into the 1940s anthropologists studying "primitive" cultures or engaged in "salvage" of aboriginal Amerindian "memory cultures" considered the study of peasants—and, even more, any study of "post-peasants" who had migrated to towns or cities in search of economic opportunity—to be sociology rather than anthropology. Eventually, there was "increasing understanding that so-called primitive or non-Western enclaves within large complex polities have been neither so primitive nor so insulated as they have often been represented in anthropological studies to be" (Mintz 1981:428). This approach became paradigmatic in the 1980s in American anthropology, although a pre-Redfieldian view continues to be espoused by some anthropologists, who see a singular Chinese civilization (for example, Cohen 1990:119; M. Wolf 1992).

15. Gates (1987:232) later acknowledged that the Japanese wished to "Japanize the Taiwanese" and that the impact of Japanese control has been underestimated. She also stressed that "we must demonstrate continuities [with the Chinese past], not assume them." She had earlier faulted Burton Pasternak's naïveté in dismissing the importance of Japanese influences on Taiwanese social structure (Rohsenow 1973b:78). On Japanese education on Taiwan and the effort to promote the Japanese language through education in Japanese, see Sugimoto 1971.

16. Interestingly, the title of the first sustained discourse on Taiwan in English, the entirely fraudulent George Psalmanazar's 1704 *An Historical and Geographical Description of Formosa, an Island Subject to the Emperor of Japan*, shows how little-established in European views was the subordination of the island to Qing emperors. In discussing this book, Rodney Needham (1985:90) noted that there was an

1896 reprinting (by Kegan Paul in London) of that curious piece of ethnographic fiction that included no indication that it was fictitious and had been retracted in a posthumous publication by its author.

17. Chen Chi Lu (1971:64) made a similar claim.

18. Donald Nonini reminded us of this.

19. Julian Steward (1950) made a searing pioneering critique of the application of simplistic anthropological assumptions about cultural homogeneity. Rather, a lot of anthropological assertions have come from atypical and very "marginal natives." See Kluckhohn 1943, 1945a:99, 138–45; Cannizzo 1983; Murray 1983, 1988.

20. For example, Wallace 1952; Hart 1954. Cf. the more mainstream homogeneity of each of the five cultures in longtime contact that were contrasted in Clyde Kluckhohn's study of values (eventually edited and published by Vogt and Albert in 1966).

21. Or beyond—M. Suzuki (1976:259) related twentieth-century Taiwanese *dang-gi* directly back to the epoch of the Warring States in ancient China.

22. On the complicated partial sinification and (after the communist takeover) retribalization of those Hsu studied, see Wu 1990. Hsu noted that some traits considered outside China as typical of traditional China have become part of the self-identification as non-Chinese in Yunnan (as in Taiwan in opposition to another modernizing regime opposed to "feudal superstitions"). Hsu recurrently dismissed variance within a very broad conception of Chinese essence (see Murray 2002).

23. Even the southeast China from which Taiwanese ancestors emigrated is dubiously traditional China or even Han. See H. Siu 1993.

24. Aside from the un-Taiwaneseness of "Hsin Hsing" as a place-name, the Chinese characters on the cover of the book skip from "Hsin Hsing" to the subtitle without including the characters for Taiwan. Rita Gallin (1992, personal communication) told me that Xin Xing was **a** name, though not a usually used official name, of the village.

25. There are also examples from Taiwan in Kleinman's later paradigm's exemplar, *The Illness Narratives* (1988). We have not found any Kleinman publication with *Taiwan* or *Taiwanese* in the title, including the chapter titles in Kleinman (1980), but, within his work and that of other medical anthropologists, it is much easier to tell when data from Taiwan is being discussed than in the literature on "Chinese religion" based on fieldwork on Taiwan.

26. On dangers of essentializing "Chinese medicine" and "patient," see Farquhar 1987.

27. However, Kleinman et al. forced Taiwanese data into the dubious etic domain of "medicine." I found it hard to believe the claim by Kleinman (1988:219) that Taiwanese *dang-gi* "use the term 'client,' *k'e-jen*, literally, 'guest.'" Aside from *k'e-jen* being a Beijinghua term (rather than the Hokkien *lang-kheh*), it is too mercantile and not sufficiently reverent. Inquiries to devotees of a Dailam *dang-gi* from across Taiwan in 1992 confirmed that my skepticism was justified, that *k'e-jen* is irreverent, and that the proper term is *sin-tô* (follower). Bruce Holbrook (1977)

challenged *dang-gi* being considered part of the same domain as *se-I-sian*) (Western-style doctor) and *diong-I-sian* (Chinese-style doctor). He also rejected Kleinman's folk/professional dichotomy, arguing that "there are no native terms for these mystically cognized categories" (151; criticizing specifically Kleinman 1975). On the problematic conceptual status of "professional" more generally, see Roth 1974.

It bears noting that Holbrook did not satisfactorily establish the emic salience of his own favored domain "Chinese medicine" including "real" and "fake" Chinese doctors, either. Just as, despite the preoccupation of anthropologists with kinship, the full set of Taiwanese kinship terms has not been published, there is no emically warranted typology of whatever the emic domain closest to the etic domain "medicine" may be, despite the volume of work on Taiwanese healers and clients. This is elaborated in chap. 8.

28. Emphasizing intracultural diversity, Kleinman and his followers rejected the quest for the formal native taxonomies of mutually exclusive, tightly integrated, hierarchically arranged categories and for uniquely derivable native diagnoses in the ethnoscience tradition exemplified by Frake (1961). Kleinman (1975) launched an all-out attack on one attempt at ethnoscientific analysis of healers on Taiwan (Holbrook 1974) but blandly absorbed some ethnoscientific work in the background to his synthesis of clinical and cultural analysis (for example, see Kleinman 1980:30). In general, as Murray (1982) suggested, ethnoscience dissolved into various cognitive anthropologies rather than being destroyed by criticism.

29. As Judith Farquhar (1990, personal communication) pointed out, the heavy repetition of some Taiwanese terms, notably *tang-ki* (*dang-gi*), gives the appearance that Kleinman used more native terms than he did in writing about the research he did on Taiwan. For instance, from Kleinman 1980:218, the six underlined *tang-ki* jump out at the reader, but he used (more discreetly italicized) Beijinghua terms for the symptoms of "depressed" and "anxious" rather than what the Taiwanese consulting the *dang-gi* used to label the problems about which they sought help from the possessing deity.

30. A notable example is Marcel Griaule's (1965) *Conversations with Ogotemmêli*.

31. For example, Williams 1988; Mueller 1977; Fei, Ranis, and Kuo 1979; Kuo, Ranis, and Fei 1981; Barrett and Whyte 1982. There is one mention of Taipei pollution in the generally laudatory account of urbanization of Speare et al. (1988:192). Ho (1978:230) noted that air pollution doubled in residential areas of Daiba between 1959 and 1965 and commented: "For those living in Daiba and its vicinity the quality of life has been adversely affected by this development—a change not taken into account by the per capita consumption indicator" (or other conventional indicators of development). Cheng (1989:499) noted the increasing salience of environmental concerns in Taiwan; Kim (200a) noted the greater tie to dissident politics of the environmental movement in Taiwan in contrast to that in South Korea. Also see Williams 1989; Bello and Rosenfeld 1990; Weller 2000:111–25; and the massive Academia Sinica steering committee's report, *Taiwan 2000: Balancing Economic Growth and Environmental Protection*.

32. The government of the Republic of China, about which she was writing was anything but "Taiwanese." Although I advocate clear distinction of *Taiwanese* from *Chinese*, the government on Taiwan circa 1984 was a Chinese oligarchy.

## 8. A Woman Who Became a Spirit Medium

Page reference without author or year in this and the next chapter are to Wolf 1992.

1. Huang (1990:33) rejected "pollution" as a Taiwanese or Chinese concept and accused Ahern of twisting data to fit an a priori Western feminist mold, supplementing Yu's (1986) critique of other theory-driven distortions in Ahern's account of Chinan (Q'inan).

2. Besides obliterating her name with the pseudonym "Wu Chieh," Wolf (1992) supplies very little information about the young Taiwanese woman who gathered most of the materials on the case Wolf tells in various ways. The reason to suppose that "Wu Chieh" was a Christian is that another longtime Wolf assistant told me that he was recruited originally through a Christian organization in the capital (Huang Chiehshan, 1989 interview). Christians on Taiwan (Chinese and Taiwanese), particularly converts, are often actively hostile to native polytheism and religious pluralism.

3. Given that a major part of Wolf's (1990, 1992) argument (taken up in the next chapter) is that Taiwanese women's names are obliterated, her decision to obliterate the name of the Taiwanese woman who wrote the second of the three tellings of the tale of the woman who did not become a *dang-gi* is especially ironic.

4. Taiwanese consider grotesque deaths, especially death throes involving simultaneous bleeding from eyes, ears, nose, and mouth (*chit-khong chhut hoeh*, seven-hole bleeding), important indicators of cosmic disfavor. The extent to which this disfavor is with a particular individual (in contrast to his or her family) could be debated.

5. Regional endogamy is normative and village endogamy common. The reputation of A-Koan's father may have made marriage brokers and local families with marriageable men wary.

6. This was before the 1996 change in the law that made the "best interest of the child" the primary consideration for deciding custody and greatly increased the awarding of (usually exclusive) custody to mothers (see Liu 2001).

7. Despite their origin in China, most—one of my nephews, who has a special interest in such matters, estimated nine out of ten—gods and goddesses speaking through *dang-gi* in Taiwan speak in Holo, albeit at times less than clearly and often with some incomprehensible words and phrases. Akinnaso (1992:98) characterizes the language of divination as similar to written, technical language in that "both kinds of languages are institutionalized, authoritarian, stylized, detached, formal, and relatively inaccessible; are characterized by register peculiarities, archaism, esoteric lexicon, elaborated grammatical structures, and semantic density; and, consequently, are discontinuous with everyday conversational language."

The specialness of divination language does not require simultaneous differentiation from everyday talk along **all** these dimensions at the same time (reduced by Wolf [100] to an "enigmatic quality"). Guan Gong speaks through my family's *dang-gi* in a heavily accented Beijinghua, in contrast to the Holo the *dang-gi* speaks in everyday life when not possessed. Also, when not possessed, he writes awkwardly and slowly, but, when possessed, he writes with great fluidity and flourish.

8. Usually, altars are in the middle of Taiwanese dwellings. Mahzo's altar is at the end of the eastern wing in the Li house.

9. When we were growing up, we had only thin rice gruel to eat in the morning, so I was momentarily surprised that abstaining from meat in the morning could now be regarded as a reportable sacrifice to one's calling.

10. Wolf (102) counterpoised most villagers being "true believers" with hearing some cynicism like that reported in Hong Kong. I doubt that Peihotien villagers expressed doubts in public situations where followers of an established *dang-gi* were present.

11. There was no *dang-gi* living in Peihotien (102).

12. Who summoned him is unclear in both the fieldnotes and in Wolf's narratives.

13. Since the farmers' revolt of 1989 (see Hsiao 1990) led to greater rural prosperity, there is considerably more money to reward *dang-gis* than there was when I was growing up and Margery Wolf was doing fieldwork somewhat farther north in northwestern Taiwan. Also see Jordan 1972:75.

14. Murray (1994a) argues that the Western elite (feminist) distinction between *sex* and *gender* is not made in most cultures or that the expected congruity between biological sex and social gender is so close to complete that in quotidian social life this is often a distinction without a difference. "Bloody frenzy" (Suzuki 1976:258)— a more vivid characterization than Wolf's "unfeminine" (111)—does not characterize my family's male *dang-gi*, Li A-Koan, or the male *dang-gi* I remember from my childhood (or the one Gould-Martin [1975:121] described). All spoke softly. None jumped about, let alone stabbed themselves, as is common among Southeast Asian possessions (including the Singapore ones Elliott [1955] discussed and Wolf [107] extrapolated from). While resisting possession, one of my relatives stabbed himself. However, once he accepted that he was going to be recurrently possessed, he did not engage in any further bloodletting.

15. Some distinguished anthropological theorists, including Edward Sapir, Paul Radin, Clyde Kluckhohn, and Bronislaw Malinowski, sought to use native form feelings, elicited and quoted native texts, and encouraged native analysts (especially Chinese ones). Those such as A. Radcliffe-Brown and George Peter Murdock, who have most vociferously exalted the special insight of professional anthropologists, gathered little usable, reliable data on the ground (in the field). Their dismissal of native models as "ideology" itself constitutes an ideology (one of "professionalism"), distracting attention from the paucity and the deficiencies of data they gathered and their dubious interpretation of data gathered by others. Claude Lévi-

Strauss called my attention to his 1953 statement that follows his more famous one that "conscious models, which are usually known as 'norms' are by definition very poor ones, since they are not intended to explain the phenomena but to perpetuate them":

> Many "primitive" cultures have built models . . . which are more to the point than models built by professional anthropologists. . . . One cannot dispense with studying a culture's "home-made" models for two reasons. First, these models might prove to be accurate or, at least to provide some insight into the structure of the phenomenon; after all, each culture has its own theoreticians whose contributions deserve the same attention as that which anthropologists give colleagues. And, second, even if the models are biased or erroneous, the very bias and types or errors are part of the facts under study and probably rank among the most significant ones. (527)

16. In acknowledging her "total lack" of command of it, Wolf (1968:v) labeled Hokkien a "dialect," though it differs as much from Beijinghua as French does from Romanian. If Hokkien was only a different dialect, some of it should have been comprehensible to Wolf, as some of, say, Australian English is to me.

17. I am not setting myself up as the sole repository or ultimate arbiter of Taiwanese culture (or even of rural Holo Taiwanese culture during the late 1950s). My reanalysis depends as much on evidence from the field notes Wolf published as from growing up in Taiwan and discussing *dang-gis* (including Li and Tan) with other natives in our native language for 50-plus years. My reinterpretation of the case of Mrs. Tan clearly is **a** native view and is based, in ways that Wolf's analysis could not be, on native premises. It is also based, in ways that Wolf's article and book could but (judging by their acknowledgments as well as their contents) were not, on discussion of general criteria for recognizing genuine spirit possession with other native Taiwanese. This by no means guarantees that mine is the only possible view of a native Holo-speaking Taiwanese of my generation (some of whom are atheists or Christians), but, at least in regards to interpreting the behavior of Mrs. Tan, it bears mentioning that I am in accord with the village consensus that was reached in nine days in March 1960.

18. A commercial aspect to acquiring a *gim sin* is peripheral in the view of believers, and such a characterization is disrespectful of the decision to move a container of divinity to a home altar.

19. See Wolf (1992:12–14, 119–20, 123–24, her subtitle, and, indeed her entire oeuvre) on her feminist motivations for publishing various accounts of the case and of Taiwanese women usually referred to as "Chinese women" within a singular Chinese culture. *Feminist* is her self-representation (especially to Rofel 2003:596,599), not my attribution. In that Wolf (1968, 1972) used Taiwanese materials to pioneer an analysis of women's resistance to patriarchy, her arguing victimization (specifically discrimination against women in being considered *dang-gis*), rather than interpreting Mrs. Tan's "breakdowns" as protests or rebellions against her lot,

is surprising—retrograde even—given the shift in feminist discourse from arguing victimization to celebrating resistance and female agency.

20. Usually, after being broken by thoroughly adopting mothers, such girls are married to sons (see M. Wolf 1972; A. Wolf and Huang 1980). Whether this was the plan in this instance is unclear, but it seems likely because such marriages were exceptionally frequent in northwestern Taiwan during Japanese rule. Margery Wolf was unwilling or unable to recover the age at which the future Mrs. Tan was adopted when I wrote to ask her. The age at adoption, the age at which her adopted family passed her on, and the age at which she fled the family she was serving are of considerable importance in interpreting her reactions.

21. Wolf inserted in brackets here: "The family she worked for scolded her or there was something of a sexual nature." I have no doubt that her life was hard in her natal family, in the family into which she was adopted, and in the family her adopted family sent her to work for (and, finally, with her wastrel husband). "The woman who didn't become a shaman" conflates the second and third families. In her 1992 text "something happened" becomes implied rape or attempted rape (96). Although turning fieldnotes into narratives is a central concern of her book, Wolf does not explain why the fieldnote's openness to several possibilities (to which I would add a pattern of paranoia about being "bullied" and the hypersensitivity Mrs. Tan's mother noted) was closed in this way decades after the time of the fieldwork. The prominence of "child abuse" in the American zeitgeist of the 1990s seems a likely explanation, another instance of forcing data into the victimization paradigm.

22. Given Wolf's claim that women's personal identities are obliterated in Taiwan, it is somewhat paradoxical that Mrs. Tan had so much of nonconforming individuality that it got in the way of possession (or, in Wolf's view of what occurs, interfered with her ability to counterfeit possession). Moreover, Mrs. Tan's feelings of persecution, recorded early in the fieldnotes, indicate that she saw herself as a distinct entity with a particular fate and do not jibe with the nonindividuation of "Chinese" women that Wolf presses (144–45).

23. Hakka/Holo (speaker) differences have not been ignored, and speakers of the two languages are not randomly distributed through the countryside, but both Wolf's rejected would-be dang-gi and my village's accepted one are from the Holo ranks. Similarly, both are rural.

24. If, as one reviewer suggested, gender is not constant between the two cases (because women's status has risen, making them more plausible for diverse social roles), one would expect the ratio of female to male dang-gis to have risen. Not being licensed by a state (one that historically has been quite hostile to such practices and practitioners), there are no hard data, but there is not the appearance of women taking over the role that has been reported in possession cults elsewhere (including on the islands and peninsulas north of Taiwan, in Africa, and in Afro-Caribbean cults). Weller (1999:86) asserted in passing that, in the religious revival occurring in China, many of the spirit mediums now are women, almost surely

more than before the [Communist] Revolution." Although his book compares the emergence/reemergence of Taiwanese and Chinese civil society, and particularly focuses on women's roles, he did not make the same claim of increasing female dominance of the spirit medium role for Taiwan.

25. Since the initial publication of Wolf's article, there have been works by anthropologists describing experience as novices within alien belief systems, including Wafer 1991; Desjarlais 1992; Turner 1992, 1999; and Trix 1993. See Wikan 1990, 1992; and Ewing 1994 on the methodological and human gains of less antagonistic (to native beliefs and concerns) fieldwork that treats members of other communities as equals (to First World anthropologists) rather than deluded inferiors.

26. Wolf (1968:v) described her Beijinghua as "weak" at the time of the Peihotien fieldwork.

27. There is some irony in the worship of Chinese (albeit not northern Chinese) gods and goddesses serving as symbols for Taiwanese resistance to Chinese regimes, especially in the instances in which the god speaks in Beijinghua rather than Holo. Language in Taiwan, as elsewhere, is the predominant symbol and vehicle for patriotism/nationalism/ethnicity (Mendel 1970; Hsiao 1989; Lo 1994; Stafford 2000:169; cf. Anderson 1992; Woolard 1985). To complicate matters further, according to Tsuah (1989), the alien (Manchu) Qing Dynasty promoted veneration of Mahzo on Taiwan while attempting to suppress worship of Ong-Yia (the plague god), whose followers tended to be more disruptive of the social order than those of the compassionate goddess.

28. I am mindful that there is a danger of substituting a smaller, shorter-term essence "Taiwanese" for the essence "Chinese" stretched across a vast space and four millennia. Although I consider that this would still be a major analytical advance, I am (and long have been) actively concerned about making sure that native speakers of Hakka, aboriginal Austronesian languages, and (even if they identify themselves as Taiwanese) Beijinghua are included in the category *Taiwanese*, which is a label based on solidarity and self-identification, rather than on descent.

29. Status follows money (albeit incompletely and with some lag), as Max Weber long ago noted, and women's increased wage labor has increased their families' evaluation of their worth. See Diamond 1979; Farris 1989; R. Gallin 1989; Marsh 1996:46; Stafford 1992; and quantitative specifications by Mehrotra and Parish 2001; M.-C. Tseng 2001; and Xu and Lai 2002. Although the status of women rose in Taiwan between 1960 and 1990, Wolf's work seriously exaggerates the extent to which daughters circa 1960 were disconnected from their natal families and were depersonalized. See demonstrations by el-Messeri (1978), Ewing (1990), and Wikan (1980, 1990) that women's selves are not so easily obliterated in very patriarchal societies, as some have supposed.

30. An anonymous reviewer suggested as a possibly important difference between Mrs. Tan and Li A-Koan that the latter is a villager known to us from birth. I think that the folk wisdom in the Judeo-Christian maxim "No one is a prophet in his hometown" has wider generalizability and that it is harder to credit the sudden

religious vocation of someone one has always known than that of an outsider whose ordinariness has not been taken for granted as long. Distance from and degree of contact with natal home is important for assessing stress on Taiwanese women—but does not seem relevant to evaluating whether one is possessed and, if so, by deities or by ghosts. Thus, this factor would seem to militate against the acceptance of Li's vocation and celestial connections.

31. Semantic analysis sometimes presses natives to focus on drawing category boundaries for instances that they generally do not try to distinguish clearly, while some neo-Durkheimian analysis focuses on dramatizing boundaries. See Brown 1976; Kay 1978; Rosch 1977; Murray 1983b, 1986, 1994b:366–69.

### 9. The Non-Obliteration of Women's Names

1. Marriage (Cantonese *hao*) names for men, Watson (1986:625) rightly notes, are not popular in Taiwan, except among high government officials trying to emulate the profusion of names Sun Yat-Sen employed.

2. Names are assigned shortly after birth, since births must be registered promptly. Personal names have meaning, that is, are not arbitrary (see Akinnaso 1982). Taiwanese and Chinese personal names are as variegated as the store of surnames is limited. Negative names to protect infants from spirits who might want to take them away are not used (cf. Akinnaso 1980, 1982:59).

3. Wang Yichun told us that the gravestones of Hakka wives do not include their personal names. In that Hakka women have historically been seen as having greater autonomy than Holo women (foot binding being a compelling indicator), this is another reversal of the relationship between status and naming Wolf proposes, if it is so.

4. In addition to adding a compelling example, Jacquemet (1992:n. 9) quotes some canonical statements of the distinction. For the relevance of the distinction on the islands immediately north of Taiwan, see T. Suzuki (1978:102–13). On denigrating forms of address to (American) females, see Gardner 1980.

5. For complications of differing status and consideration of a general historical trend to reciprocity in forms of address, see Brown and Gilman 1960; Murray 1978; and Kroger and Wood 1992.

6. This is probably also the case for rural mainland China; Huang (1990:21) documented roles for mother's natal families in contemporary Shandong. Huang (1990:33) accused another leading feminist anthropologist, Emily Ahern (Martin) (1978) of twisting data to fit a priori Western assumptions about women's "pollution," supplementing Yu's (1986) critique of other theory-driven distortions in Ahern's account of Q'inan, the northwestern Taiwanese village in which she did fieldwork.

### 10. The Aftermath

1. For example, M. Brown 1996, 2001, 2003, 2004; H. Chen 1992; Ch'en, Chuang, and Huang 1994; Chi 2000; Chu 2000; Chun 2000a, 2002; Corcuff 2000,

2002; Dreyer 2003; Hsiau 2003; Kuo 2002; T.-H. Lee 1999; Pan 1994; Simon 2003a; F. Wang 1994. 2002a, b; H.-L. Wang 2000; Wong 2001; D. Wu 1997; You 1994; N. Wu 2002; Yu 1996. The only anthropologist in this now-licit discourse (Brown) has been investigating the Hanification of Aborigines, mostly in the Japanese colonial era, while the rest address cultural and political meanings of Taiwanese/Mainlander contrasts. Wang Fu-Chang (2002b) found that the highest amount of ethnic consciousness typified the Mainlanders (early generations of whom made a Chinese/Taiwanese distinction extremely salient for those in the latter disprivileged group). Using data collected from several sets of nationwide house interview surveys, Wu Nai-Teh (2002) showed that for ethnic politics there is not a cleavage between Hakka and Holo speakers but only one between Mainlanders and Taiwanese (the latter including Mainlander progeny identifying as "new Taiwanese" rather than as "Chinese"; also see M. Li 2003).

2. Sociologist Robert Marsh (2003) provided data from representative national surveys conducted in 1992 and 1997 that Taiwanese mean (self-reported) level of participation in fifteen types of formal voluntary organizations was not only much lower than that in the United States (and several other societies) but declined significantly between 1992 and 1997, as democracy was advancing. Unlike Weller and M.-H. Yang (2002), Marsh analyzed the recent Taiwanese past without trying to predict the Chinese future.

### Acknowledgments

1. I would think that "reverse Orientalism" would be non-Westerners such as myself exoticizing a unitary "West."

# References

Ahern, Emily M.

    1975   Sacred and Secular Medicine in a Taiwan Village. *In* Medicine in Chinese Cultures. Arthur Kleinman et al., eds. Pp. 91–113. Washington: U.S. Government Printing Office.

    1978   The Power and Pollution of Chinese Women. *In* Studies in Chinese Society. Arthur Wolf, ed. Pp. 269–90. Stanford: Stanford University Press.

Ahern, Emily M., and Hill Gates

    1981   The Anthropology of Taiwanese Society. Stanford: Stanford University Press.

Akinnaso, F. Niyi

    1980   The Sociolinguistic Basis of Yoruba Personal Names. Anthropological Linguistics 22:275–304.

    1982   Names and Naming in Cross-Cultural Perspective. Names 30:37–63.

    1992   Schooling, Language, and Knowledge in Literate and Nonliterate Societies. Comparative Studies in Society and History 34:68–109.

Amsden, Alice

    1979   Taiwan's Economic History: A Case of Étatisme and a Challenge to Dependency Theory. Modern China 5:341–79.

Anderson, Benedict R. O'G.

    1992   Imagined Communities: Reflections on the Origin and Spread of Nationalism. London: Verso.

Anderson, Perry

    2004   Hypotheses on Taiwanese Nationalism. Presentation at the University of California, Los Angeles, Center for Chinese Studies, 13 May. Online summary at www.international.ucla.edu/ccs/article.asp?parentid=11244.

Appell, Laura W. R., and George N. Appell

    1993   To Do Battle with the Spirits: Bulusu Spirit Mediums. *In* The Seen and the Unseen: Shamanism, Mediumship and Possession in Borneo. Robert Winzler, ed. Pp. 55–99. Williamsburg VA: Borneo Research Council.

Asad, Talal

 1973 Anthropology and the Colonial Encounter. London: Ithaca Press.

 1986 The Concept of Cultural Translation in British Social Anthropology. *In* Writing Culture. J. Clifford & G. Marcus, eds. Pp. 141–64. Berkeley: University of California Press.

Atkinson, Jane Mannig

 1992 Shamanism Today. Annual Review of Anthropology 21:307–30.

Baity, Philip C.

 1975 Religion in a Chinese Town. Taipei: Orient Culture Service.

Balzer, Marjorie Mandelstam

 1987 Behind Shamanism. Social Science and Medicine 24:1085–93.

 1990 Shamanism. Armonk NY: M. E. Sharpe.

Barclay, George W.

 1954 Colonial Development and Population in Taiwan. Princeton NJ: Princeton University Press.

Barnhart, Terry A.

 2005 Ephraim George Squier and the Development of American Anthropology. Lincoln: University of Nebraska Press.

Barrett, Richard E.

 1990 Seasonality in Vital Processes in a Traditional Chinese Population: Births, Deaths, and Marriages in Colonial Taiwan, 1906–1942. Modern China 16:190–225.

Barrett, Richard E., and Martin K. Whyte

 1982 Dependency Theory and Taiwan: A Deviant Case Analysis. American Journal of Sociology 87:1064–89.

Barth, Fredrik

 1993 Balinese Worlds. Chicago: University of Chicago Press.

Beardsley, Richard K.

 1954 Community Studies in Japan. Far Eastern Quarterly 14:37–55.

Bello, Walden, and Stephanie Rosenfeld

 1990 Dragons in Distress: Asia's Miracle Economies in Crisis. San Francisco: Institute for Food and Development Policy.

Bennett, John W.

 1998 Classic Anthropology. New Brunswick NJ: Transaction.

Bernard, H. Russell

 1992 Preserving Language Diversity. Human Organization 51:82–89.

Bernstein, Jay H.

 1993 The Shaman's Destiny: Symptoms, Affliction, and the Reinterpretation of Illness among the Taman. *In* The Seen and the Unseen: Shamanism, Mediumship and Possession in Borneo. Robert Winzler, ed. Pp. 171–206. Williamsburg VA: Borneo Research Council.

Besmer, Fremont E.

    1983   Horses, Musicians, and Gods: The Hausa Cult of Possession-Trance. Zaria, Nigeria: Ahmadu Bello University Press.

Bessac, Frank B.

    1964   Some Social Effects of Land Reform in a Village on the Taichung Plain. Journal of the China Society 4:15–28.

    1967   An Example of Social Change in Taiwan Related to Land Reform. University of Montana Contributions to Anthropology 1:1–31.

Bieder, Robert E.

    1986   Science Encounters the Indian, 1820–1880: The Early Years of American Ethnology. Norman: University of Oklahoma Press.

Boddy, Janice

    1994   Spirit Possession Revisited: Beyond Instrumentality. Annual Reviews in Anthropology 21:407–34.

Bodman, Nicholas Cleaveland

    1955   Spoken Amoy Hokkien. Kuala Lumpar, Malaya: Federation of Malaya Government Officers' Language School.

Bosco, Joseph

    1992a   The Emergence of Taiwanese Popular Culture. American Journal of Chinese Studies 1:51–56.

    1992b   Taiwan Factions: Guanxi, Patronage, and the State in Local Politics. Ethnology 31:157–83.

Bourguignon, Erika

    1973   Religion, Altered States of Consciousness, and Social Change. Columbus: Ohio State University Press.

    1991a   Possession. Prospect Heights IL: Waveland Press.

    1991b   A. Irving Hallowell, the Foundations of Psychological Anthropology and Altered States of Consciousness. Psychoanalytical Study of Society 16:17–42.

Brown, Melissa J.

    1996   Negotiating Ethnicities in China and Taiwan. (Berkeley: Center for Chinese Studies) China Research Monograph 46.

    2001   Reconstructing Ethnicity: Recorded and Remembered Identity in Taiwan. Ethnology 40:153–64.

    2003   The Cultural Impact of Gendered Social Roles and Ethnicity: Changing Religious Practices in Taiwan. Journal of Anthropological Research 59:47–67.

    2004   Is Taiwan Chinese? The Impact of Culture, Power, and Migration on Changing Identities. Berkeley Series in Interdisciplinary Studies of China 2. Berkeley: University of California Press.

Brown, Roger

    1976   Reference. Cognition 4:125–33.

Brown, Roger, and Albert Gilman

1960  The Pronouns of Power and Solidarity. *In* Style in Language. Thomas Sebeok. Pp. 253–76. Cambridge MA: MIT Press.

Cannizzo, Jeanne

1983  George Hunt and the Invention of Kwakiutl Culture. Canadian Review of Sociology and Anthropology 20:44–58.

Chang Chin-Fen

2002  Bringing the Culture Back In: The Gendered Processes within Institutions and Structures in Taiwanese Labor Markets. Taiwanese Journal of Sociology 29:97–125.

Chang Han-Pi

1997  Taiwan: Community of Fate and Cultural Globalization. New Brunswick NJ: Transaction Publishers.

Chang Kung-Chi

1986  Discerning the Multiple Cosmologies and Identifying Their Interrelationship in a Tangki's Divinatory Process. Bulletin of the Institute of Ethnology, Academia Sinica 61:81–103.

Chang Ly-Yun

1992  Medical Care as Ritual and Myth. Bulletin of the Institute of Ethnology, Academia Sinica. 74:63–93.

Chao Yuen-Ren

1956  Chinese Terms of Address. Language 32:217–41.

Chen Chi Lu

1971  The Taiwanese Family. Journal of the China Society 7:64–69.

Ch'en Chung-Min

1977  Upper Camp: A Study of a Chinese Mixed-Cropping Village in Taiwan. Taipei: Institute of Ethnology, Academia Sinica.

Ch'en Chung-Min, Chuang Ying-Chang, and Huang Shu-Min

1994  Ethnicity in Taiwan: Social, Historical, and Cultural Perspectives. Taipei: Institute of Ethnology, Academia Sinica.

Chen Hsi-Huang

1975  Economic Analysis of Small Farms. *In* Essays on Taiwan's Agricultural Development. T. Yu and Y. Yu, eds. Pp. 378–89. Daiba: Lien Ching.

Chen Hsiang-Shui

1977  Land Reform in Green-Tree Village. Bulletin of the Institute of Ethnology, Academia Sinica 43:65–84.

1992  Chinatown No More: Taiwan Immigrants in Contemporary New York. Ithaca NY: Cornell University Press.

Chen Shao-Hsing

1966  Taiwan as a Laboratory for the Study of Chinese Society and Culture. Bulletin of the Institute of Ethnology, Academia Sinica 22:1–14.

Cheng Tun-Jen

1989    Democratizing the Quasi-Leninist Regime in Taiwan. World Politics 41:471–99.

Cheng Tun-Jen, and Stephan Haggard

1992    Political Change in Taiwan. Boulder CO: Lynne Rienner.

Chi Jou-Juo

2000    Nationalism and Self-Determination: The Identity Politics in Taiwan. Journal of Asian and African Studies 35:303–21.

Ching, Leo T.

2001    Becoming "Japanese": Colonial Taiwan and the Politics of Identity Formation. Berkeley: University of California Press.

Cho Sungnam

1989    The Emergence of a Health Insurance System in a Developing Country. Journal of Health and Social Behavior. 30:467–71.

Chu Jou-Juo

2000    Nationalism and Self-Determination: The Identity Politics in Taiwan. Journal of Asian and African Studies 35:303–21.

Chuang Ying-Chang

1987    Ching Dynasty Chinese Immigration to Taiwan. Bulletin of the Institute of Ethnology, Academia Sinica 64:179–203.

1988    Settlement Patterns of the Hakka Migration to Taiwan. Bulletin of the Institute of Ethnology, Academia Sinica 34:85–98.

Chun, Allen

2000a    Democracy as Hegemony, Globalization as Indigenization, or the "Culture" in Taiwanese National Politics. Journal of Asian and African Studies 35:7–27.

2000b    From Text to Context: How Anthropology Makes Its Subject. Cultural Anthropology 15:570–95.

2002    The Coming Crisis of Multiculturalism in "Transnational" Taiwan. Social Analysis 46:102–22.

Clark, Cal

1989    Taiwan's Development: Implications for Contending Political Economy Paradigms. New York: Greenwood.

Cohen, Myron L.

1990    Being Chinese: The Peripheralization of Traditional Identity. Dædalus 120(2):113–35. (Reprinted in The Living Tree: The Changing Meaning of Being Chinese Today. W. Tu, ed. Pp. 88–108. Stanford: Stanford University Press, 1994.)

Cole, Sally

2003    Ruth Landes. Lincoln: University of Nebraska Press.

Corcuff, Stéphane

2000    Taiwan's "Mainlander": A New Ethnic Category. China Perspective 28:71–81.

2002    Memories of the Future: National Identity Issues and the Search for a New Taiwan. Armonk NY: M. E. Sharpe.

Darnell Regna

1971a    The Powell Classification of American Indian Languages. Papers in Linguistics 4:90–110.

1971b    The Revision of the Powell Classification. Papers in Linguistics 4:233–57.

1977    Hallowell and "Bear Ceremonialism." Ethos 5:13–30.

1998    And Along Came Boas: Continuity and Revolution in Americanist Anthropology. Amsterdam: John Benjamins.

2001    Invisible Genealogies: A History of Americanist Anthropology. Lincoln: University of Nebraska Press.

Davidson, James W.

1903    The Island of Formosa. New York: Macmillan (reprinted by Oxford University Press, 1988).

De Glopper, Donald R.

1974    Religion and Ritual in Lukang. In A. Wolf 1974:43–69.

1977    Old Medicine in a New Bottle. Reviews in Anthropology 4:349–59.

1995    Lukang: Commerce and Community in a Chinese City. (Revised version of 1973 Cornell PhD diss., "City on the Sands: Social Structure in a Nineteenth-Century Chinese City".) Albany: State University of New York Press.

Desjarlais, Robert R.

1992    Body and Emotions: The Aesthetics of Illness and Healing in Nepal. Philadelphia: University of Pennsylvania Press.

Diamond, Norma

1969    K'un Shen, A Taiwan Village. New York: Holt, Rinehart and Winston.

1979    Women in Industry in Taiwan. Modern China 5:317–40.

DiGiacomo, Susan M.

2002    Translation and/as Ethnographic Practice. Anthropology News 43(5):10.

Dreyer, June Teufel

2003    Taiwan's Evolving Identity. In The Evolution of Taiwanese National Identity. Pp. 4–10. Woodrow Wilson International Center Special Report (August).

Eberhard, Wolfram

1967    Settlement and Change in Asia. Hong Kong University Press.

1970    Studies in Chinese Folklore and Related Essays, Indiana University Folklore Institute Monograph 23.

Eliade, Mircea

1951    Le chamanisme et les techniques archaiques de l'extase. Paris: Payot.

Elliot, Alan J. A.

    1955   Chinese Spirit Medium Cults in Singapore. London: London School of Economics and Political Science.

el-Messiri, Saswan

    1978   Self-Images of Traditional Urban Women in Cairo. *In* Women in the Muslim World. L. Beck and N. Keddie, eds. Pp. 522–40. Cambridge MA: Harvard University Press.

Elvin, Mark

    1985   Between the Earth and Heaven: Conceptions of the Self in China. *In* The Category of the Person. Michael Carrithers, Steven Collins, and Steven Lukes, eds. Pp. 156–89. Cambridge: Cambridge University Press.

Embree, John F.

    1939   Suye Mura. Chicago: University of Chicago Press.

Ewing, Katherine P.

    1990   The Illusion of Wholeness. Ethos 18:251–78.

    1994   Dreams from a Saint: Anthropological Atheism and the Temptation to Believe. American Anthropologist 96:571–83.

Farmer, Paul, and Arthur Kleinman

    1989   AIDS as Human Suffering. Dædalus 118(2):135–60.

Farris, Catherine S.

    1988   Gender and Grammar in Chinese with Implications for Language Universals. Modern China 14:277–308.

    1989   The Social Discourse on Women's Roles in Taiwan. Journal of Oriental Studies 27:76–92.

Farquhar, Judith

    1987   Problems of Knowledge in Contemporary Chinese Medical Discourse. Social Science and Medicine 24:1013–21.

Fei Hsiao-Tung (Xiaotong)

    1939   Peasant Life in China: A Field Study of Country Life in the Yangtze Valley. London: Kegan Paul.

Fei Hsiao-Tung and Chang Chih-I (Zhang Zhiyi)

    1945   Earthbound China: A Study of Rural Economy in Yunnan. Chicago: University of Chicago Press.

Fei, John C. H., Gustav Ranis, and Shirley W. Y. Kuo.

    1979   Growth with Equity: The Taiwan Case. Washington DC: World Bank.

Feng H.-Y.

    1936   Teknonymy as a Formative Factor in the Chinese Kinship System. American Anthropologist 38:59–66.

Feuchtwang, Stephan

    1992   The Imperial Metaphor: Popular Religion in China. London: Routledge.

Fichte, Hubert

    1985   Lazarus und die Waschmaschine. Frankfurt a/M: Fischer.

Fidler, Richard C.

    1993   Spirit Possession as Exculpation with Examples from the Sarawak Chinese. *In* The Seen and the Unseen: Shamanism, Mediumship and Possession in Borneo. Robert Winzler, ed. Pp. 207–32. Williamsburg VA: Borneo Research Council.

Firth, Raymond

    1959   Problem and Assumption in the Anthropological Study of Religion. Journal of the Royal Anthropological Institute 89:129–48.

Foerstel, Lenora, and Angela Gilliam

    1992   Confronting the Margaret Mead Legacy: Scholarship, Empire, and the South Pacific. Philadelphia: Temple University Press.

Fond, Vanessa L.

    2002   China's One-Child Policy and the Empowerment of Urban Daughters. American Anthropologist 104:1098–1109.

Form, William

    2002   Work and Academic Politics. New Brunswick NJ: Transaction.

Frake, Charles O.

    1961   Diagnosis of Disease among the Subanun of Mindanao. American Anthropologist 63:113–32.

Fried, Morton

    1954   Community Studies: China. Far Eastern Quarterly 14:11–36.

Friedman, Edward

    1993   A Failed Chinese Modernity. Dædalus 122(2):1–17.

Fry, Peter

    1976   Spirits of Protest. Cambridge: Cambridge University Press.

Gallin, Bernard

    1963   Land Reform in Taiwan: Its Effect on Rural Social Organization and Leadership. Human Organization 22:109–22.

    1964   Rural Development in Taiwan: The Role of the Government. Rural Sociology 29:313–23.

    1966   Hsin Hsing, Taiwan. Berkeley: University of California Press.

    1975   Comments on Contemporary Sociocultural Studies of Medicine in Chinese Societies. *In* Medicine in Chinese Cultures. Arthur Kleinman et al., eds. Pp. 273–80. Washington DC: U.S. Government Printing Office.

Gallin, Bernard, and Rita S. Gallin

    1974a   The Integration of Village Migrants in Taipei. *In* The Chinese City between Two Worlds. M. Elvin and G. Skinner, eds. Pp. 331–58. Stanford: Stanford University Press.

    1974b   The Rural-to-Urban Migration of Anthropologists in Taiwan. *In* Anthropologists in Cities. G. Foster and R. Kemper, eds. Pp. 223–48. Boston: Little, Brown.

Gallin, Rita S.

    1983   Women at Work in Hsin Hsing. Taiwan Review (spring): 12–15.

    1984   The Entry of Chinese Women into the Rural Labor Force: A Case Study from Taiwan. Signs 9:383–98.

    1989   Women and Work in rural Taiwan. Journal of Health and Social Behavior 30:374–85.

    1992   Wife Abuse in the Context of Development and Change: A Chinese [Taiwanese] Case. *In* Sanctions and Sanctuary: Cultural Perspectives on the Beating of Wives. D. Counts, J. Brown, and J. Campbell, eds. Pp. 219–27. Boulder: Westview Press.

Gardner, Carol Brooks

    1980   "Passing By": Street Remarks, Address Rights and the Urban [U.S.] Female. Sociological Inquiry 50:328–56.

Gates, Hill

    1979   Dependency and the Part-Time Proletariat in Taiwan." Modern China 5:381–407.

    1981   Ethnicity and Social Class. *In* The Anthropology of Taiwanese Society. E. Ahern and H. Gates, eds. Pp. 241–81. Stanford: Stanford University Press.

    1987   Chinese Working Class Lives. Ithaca NY: Cornell University Press.

    1997   China's Motor: A Thousand Years of Petty Capitalism. Ithaca NY: Cornell University Press.

    1999   Looking for Chengdu: A Woman's Adventures in China. Ithaca NY: Cornell University Press.

Gellner, Ernest

    1983   Nations and Nationalism. New York: Blackwell.

Geertz, Clifford

    1959   Form and Variation in Balinese Village Structure. American Anthropologist 61:991–1012.

Giles, Linda L.

    1987   Possession Cults on the Swahili Coast: A Re-examination of Theories of Marginality. Africa 57:234–54.

Gold, Thomas B.

    1986   State and Society in the Taiwan Miracle. Armonk NJ: M. E. Sharpe.

    1994   Civil Society and Taiwan's Quest for Identity. *In* Harrell and Huang 1994:47–68.

    1996   Civil Society in Taiwan: The Confucian Dimension. *In* Confucian Traditions in East Asian Modernities. Tu Wei-Ming, ed. Pp. 244–58. Cambridge MA: Harvard University Press.

    2003   Identity and Symbolic Power in Taiwan. *In* The Evolution of Taiwanese National Identity. Pp. 11–16. Woodrow Wilson International Center Special Report (August).

Goldschmidt, Walter

 1985   The Cultural Paradigm in the Post-War World. *In* Social Contexts
 of American Ethnology, 1840–1984. June Helm, ed. Pp. 164–76. Washington DC: American Anthropological Association.

 1997   Foreword: The End of Peasantry. *In* Farewell to Peasant China. G.
 Guldin, ed. Pp. vii–xv. Armonk NY: M. E. Sharpe.

Gould-Martin, Katherine

 1975   Medical Systems in a Taiwan Village: *Ong-Ia-Kong*, The Plague God
 as Modern Physician in Taiwan. *In* Medicine in Chinese Cultures. Arthur
 Kleinman et al., eds. Pp. 115–40. Washington: U.S. Government Printing
 Office.

Grajdanzev, Andrew J.

 1942   Formosa Today. New York: Institute of Pacific Research.

Granovetter, Mark S.

 1985   Economic Action and Social Structure: The Problem of Embed-
 dedness. American Journal of Sociology 91:481–510.

Grayson, Benjamin Lee

 1979   The American Image of China. New York: Ungar.

Griaule, Marcel

 1965   Conversations with Ogotemmêli. London: International African
 Institute.

Guldin, Gregory E.

 1994   The Saga of Anthropology in China: From Malinowski to Moscow
 to Mao. Armonk NY: M. E. Sharpe.

Haller, Dietrich

 2001   Reflections on the Merits and Perils of Insider Anthropology.
 Zietschrift für Kulturwissenschaften 14:113–46.

Handler, Richard

 1988   Nationalism and the Politics of Culture in Québec. Madison:
 University of Wisconsin Press.

Harrell, Stevan, and Huang Chun-Chieh

 1994   Cultural Change in Post-War Taiwan. Boulder CO: Westview.

Harrer, Heinrich

 1996 [1953]   Seven Years in Tibet. New York: Putnam.

Hart, C. W. M.

 1954   The Sons of Turimpi. American Anthropologist 56:242–61.

Ho Ming-Sho

 2001   The Origin of Taiwan's Environmental Movement: Scholar-
 Experts, Political Opposition and Grassroots, 1980–1986. Taiwanese
 Sociology 2001:97–162.

Ho, Samuel P. S.

 1978   The Economic Development of Taiwan, 1860–1970. New Haven:
 Yale University Press.

Ho Szu-Yin and Liu I-Chou

    2002   The Chinese/Taiwanese Identity of the Taiwan People in the 1990s. American Asian Review 20(2):29–74.

Holbrook, Bruce

    1974   Chinese Psycho-Social Medicine: Doctor and Tang-ki, an Intercultural Analysis. Bulletin of the Institute of Ethnology, Academia Sinica 37:85–112.

    1977   Ethnoscience and Chinese Medicine, Genuine and Spurious. Bulletin of the Institute of Ethnology, Academia Sinica 43:129–80.

Holmberg David H.

    1989   Order in Paradox: Myth, Ritual and Exchange among Nepal's Tamang. Ithaca NY: Cornell University Press.

Hong Keelung

    1992   How I Became Taiwanese and Why It Matters. Keynote address to the national meeting of the Taiwanese-American Citizen's League held at Mills College, Oakland, California.

    1994   Experiences of Being a "Native" Observing Anthropology. Anthropology Today 10(3):6–9.

    2003   My Search for 2/28. Presented at a 2/28 Memorial at the University of California, Berkeley. Online at http://www.wufi.org/activities/mandarin/022803.html.

Hong Keelung and Stephen O. Murray

    1989   Complicity with Domination. American Anthropologist 91:1028–30.

    1993   Ethnographic Irresponsibility. Taiwan Typhoon 3(4):4–6.

Hou Chi-Ming

    1978   Human Resources Mobilization of a Developing Society: Labor Utilization in Taiwan. Asian Thought and Society 3:131–34.

Hsiao, Hsin-Huang Michael

    1981   Government Agricultural Strategies in Taiwan and South Korea: A Macrosociological Assessment. Institute of Ethnology, Academia Sinica Monograph 9.

    1988   An East Asian Development Model: Empirical Explorations. In In Search of an East Asian Development Model. Peter Berger and Hsin-Huang Hsiao eds. Pp. 12–23. New Brunswick NJ: Transaction.

    1989   Contemporary Intellectuals' Reflections on the Local Consciousness. In Intellectuals and the Development of Taiwan. Pp. 179–214. Taipei: Chung Kuo Lun Tan Press. (In Chinese.)

    1990   The Farmers' Movement in Taiwan in the 1980s. Bulletin of the Institute of Ethnology, Academica Sinica 70:67–94.

    1995   The State and Business Relations in Taiwan. Journal of Far Eastern Business 1:76–97.

    1998   Social Transformation, Nascent Civil Society and Taiwanese Cap-

ital in Fujian. Hong Kong Institute of Asia–Pacific Studies Occasional
Paper 84.

Hsiao Hsin-Huang, Lester Milbraith, and Robert Weller

1995   Antecedents of the Environmental Movement in Taiwan. Capitalism, Nature, Socialism 6:91–104.

Hsiau A-Chin

2003   Identity, Narrative, and Action: Anti-KMT Dissident Construction of
History in 1970s Taiwan. Taiwanese Sociology 5:195–250.

Hsieh Jih-chang and Chuang Ying-Chang

1985   The Chinese Family and Its Ritual Behavior. Daiba: Institute of
Ethnology, Academia Sinica.

Hsiung Ping-Chun

1996   Living Rooms as Factories: Class, Gender, and the Satellite Factory
System in Taiwan. Philadelphia: Temple University Press.

Hsu, Francis L. K.

1948   Under the Ancestors' Shadow. New York: Columbia University
Press.

Hsu Wen-Hsiung

1980   Frontier Social Organization and Social Disorder in Ching Taiwan.
*In* China's Island Frontier: Studies in the Historical Geography of Taiwan.
R. Knapp, ed. Pp. 87–105. Honolulu: University of Hawaii Press.

Hu Tai-Li

1984   My Mother-in-Law's Village: Rural Industrialization and Change in
Taiwan. Academia Sinica Monograph 13.

1983   Emergence of a Small-scale Industry in a Taiwanese Rural Com-
munity. *In* Women, Men, and the International Division of Labor. June
Nash and María Kelly, eds. Pp. 387–406. Albany: State University of New
York Press.

Huang Shu-Min

1981   Agricultural Degradation: Changing Community Systems in Rural
Taiwan. Lanham MD: University Press of America.

1985   Review of Ploughshare Village by Stevan Harrell. American Anthropologist 87:200–201.

1990   Folk Reproductive Medicine in North China. Bulletin of the Institute of Ethnology, Academic Sinica 70:13–38.

Hwang Chi-Lien

1968   Wages and Income of Agricultural Workers in Taiwan. Taipei:
National Taiwan University Research Institute of Rural Socio-Economics.

Ichioka, Yuji

1989   Views from Within: The Japanese American Evacuation and Resettlement Study. Los Angeles: Asian American Studies Center.

Inkeles, Alex, and Raymond A. Bauer

    1961   The Soviet Citizen: Daily Life in a Totalitarian Society. Cambridge MA: Harvard University Press.

Jackson, Jean

    1989   Is There a Way to Talk about Making Culture without Making Enemies? Dialectical Anthropology 14:127–43.

Jacquemet, Marco

    1992   Namechasers. American Ethnologist 19:733–48.

Jordan, David K.

    1972   Gods, Ghosts, and Ancestors: The Folk Religion of a Taiwanese Village. Berkeley: University of California Press.

    1994   Changes in Postwar Taiwan and Their Impact on the Popular Practice of Religion. *In* Harrell and Huang 1994:137–60.

Joyce, Barry Alan

    2001   The Shaping of American Ethnography: The Wilkes Exploring Expedition, 1838–1842. Lincoln: University of Nebraska Press.

Ka Chih-Ming

    1995   Japanese Colonialism in Taiwan. Boulder CO: Westview.

Kagan, Richard C., and Anna Wasecha

    1982   The Taiwanese Tang-ki. *In* Social Interaction in Chinese Society. S. Greenblatt, R. Wilson, and A. Wilson, eds. Pp. 112–141. New York: Praeger.

Katz, Paul R.

    2003   Religion and the State in Post-War Taiwan. China Quarterly 174:395–412.

Kay, Paul

    1978   Tahitian Words for "Class" and "Race." Publications de la Société des Océanistes 39:81–91.

Kelly, Lawrence C.

    1985   Why Applied Anthropology Developed When It Did. *In* Social Contexts of American Ethnology, 1840–1984. June Helm, ed. Pp. 122–38. Washington DC: American Anthropological Association.

Kenyatta, Jomo

    1938   Facing Mount Kenya: The Tribal Life of the Gikuyu. London: Martin Secker and Warburg.

Kerr, George H.

    1953   Ryukyu Kingdom and Province before 1945. Washington DC: Pacific Science Board, National Academy of Sciences.

    2000 [1958]   Okinawa: The History of an Island People. Rutland VT: C. E. Tuttle.

    1965   Formosa Betrayed. Boston: Houghton Mifflin.

    1974   Formosa: Licensed Revolution and the Home Rule Movement. Honolulu: University Press of Hawaii.

1986　The Taiwan Confrontation Crisis. Washington DC: Formosan Association for Public Affairs.

Kim, Sunhyuk

2000a　Democratization and Environmentalism: South Korea and Taiwan in Comparative Perspective. Journal of Asian and African Studies 35:287–302.

2000b　The Politics of Democratization in Korea: The Role of Civil Society. Pittsburgh: University of Pittsburgh Press.

Kirsch, A. T.

1977　Complexity in the Thai Religious System. Journal of Asian Studies 36:241–66.

Kitsuse, John I., and Aaron V. Cicourel

1963　A Note on the Use of Official Statistics. Social Problems 11:131–38.

Kleinman, Arthur

1975　Medical and Psychiatric Anthropology and the Study of Traditional Forms of Medicine in Modern Chinese Culture. Bulletin of the Institute of Ethnology, Academia Sinica 39:107–23.

1980　Patients and Healers in the Context of Culture. Berkeley: University of California Press.

1986　Social Origins of Distress and Disease: Depression, Neurasthenia, and Pain in Modern China. New Haven: Yale University Press.

1988　The Illness Narratives: Suffering, Healing, and the Human Condition. New York: Basic Books.

1991　Suffering and Its Professional Transformation. Culture, Medicine, and Psychiatry 15:275–301.

Kleinman, Arthur, and James L. Gale

1982　Patients Treated by Physicians and Folk Healers in Taiwan. Culture, Medicine, and Psychiatry 6:405–23.

Kluckhohn, Clyde

1943　Review of Sun Chief by Leo Simmons. American Anthropologist 45:267–70.

1945　The Personal Document in Anthropological Science. Social Science Research Council Bulletin 53:79–173.

Koo, Anthony Y.

1968　The Role of Land Reform in Economic Development: A Case Study of Taiwan. New York: Praeger.

1982　Land Market Distortion and Tenure Reform. Ames: Iowa State University Press.

Kroeber, Alfred L.

1940　Psychosis or Social Sanction? Character and Culture 8:204–15.

1948　Anthropology. New York: Harcourt, Brace, and Co.

Kroger, Rolf O., and Linda A. Wood

1992   Are Rules of Address Universal? Journal of Cross-Cultural Psychology 23:148–62.

Kung, Lydia

1984   Factory Women in Taiwan. Ann Arbor MI: UMI Research Press. (2nd ed., Columbia University Press, 1994.)

Kuo Chi-Sheng

2002   Art and Identity in Postwar Taiwan. Berlin: Peter Lang.

Kuo, Shirley W. Y., Gustav Ranis, and John C. Fei

1981   The Taiwan Success Story. Boulder CO: Westview.

Kuwayama Tkami

2003   "Natives" as Dialogic Partners: Some Thoughts on Native Anthropology. Anthropology Today 19(1):8–13.

Lai Tse-Han, Ramon H. Myers, and Wei Wou

1991   A Tragic Beginning: The Taiwan Uprising of February 28, 1947. Stanford: Stanford University Press.

Lamley, Harry J.

1970   The 1895 Taiwanese War of Resistance. In Taiwan and Its Place in Chinese History. L. Gordon, ed. Pp. 23–77. New York: Columbia University Press.

1981   Subethnic Rivalry in the Ching Period. In Ahern and Gates 1981:282–318.

Lan, David

1985   Guns and Rain: Guerrillas and Spirit Mediums in Zimbabwe. Berkeley: University of California Press.

Leach, Edmund

1964   Political Systems of Highland Burma: A Study of Kachin Social Structures. London: G. Bell.

Lee Anru

1998   The Waning of a Hard Work Ethic: Moral Discourse in Taiwan's Recent Economic Restructuring. Paper presented at the Fourth North American Taiwan Studies Conference in Austin, Texas.

2000   Stand by the Family: Gender and Taiwan's Small-scale Industry in the Global Context. Anthropology of Work Review 21(3):5–9.

Lee Teng-Hui

1999   The Road to Democracy: Taiwan's Pursuit of Identity. Tokyo: PHP Institute.

Lévi-Strauss Claude

1953   Social Structure. In Anthropology Today. Alfred Kroeber, ed. Pp. 524–53. Chicago: University of Chicago Press.

Lewis, I. M.

1971   Ecstatic Religion: An Anthropological Study of Spirit Possession and Shamanism. Harmondsworth, Eng.: Penguin.

Li Mei-chih

>2003    Bases of Ethnic Identification in Taiwan. Asian Journal of Social Psychology 6:229–37.

Li Hung Chang

>1913    Memoirs. Boston: Houghton Mifflin.

Li Thian-Hok

>2002    The Chineseness of Chen Shui-bian. Published in Taipei Times (29 April) and Taiwan Tribune (7 May).

Lin Wei-Pin

>2000    A Reconsideration of Chinese "Kinship": Ethnography of a Village in Southwestern Taiwan. Bulletin of the Institute of Ethnology Academia Sinica 90:1–38.

Lin Yueh-Hwa (Yaohua)

>1948    The Golden Wing: A Sociological Study of Chinese Familism. London: Kegan Paul.

Liu Hung-En

>2001    Mother or Father: Who Received Custody? The Best Interests of the Child Standard and Judges' Custody Decisions in Taiwan. International Journal of Law, Policy and the Family 15:185–225.

Lo Ming-Cheng

>1994    Crafting the Collective Identity: The Origin and Transformation of Taiwanese Nationalism. Journal of Historical Sociology 7:198–223.

>2003    Doctors within Borders: Profession, Ethnicity, and Modernity in Colonial Taiwan. Taiwanese Sociology 5:262–68.

Lu Hsin-Yi

>2002    The Politics of Locality: Making a Nation of Communities in Taiwan. New York: Routledge.

Lu Yu-Hsia

>2001    The "Boss's Wife" and Taiwanese Small Family Business. In Women's Working Lives in East Asia. Mary Brinton, ed. Pp. 263–97. Stanford: Stanford University Press.

Luo Zhufeng

>1991    Religion under Socialism in China. Armonk NY: M. E. Sharpe.

Marsh, Robert M.

>1996    The Great Transformation: Social Change in Taipei, Taiwan since the 1960s. Armonk NY: M. E. Sharpe.

>2003    Social Capital, Guanxi, and the Road to Democracy in Taiwan. Comparative Sociology 2:575–604.

Martin, Howard H.

>1996    The Hakka Ethnic Movement in Taiwan. In Guest People: Hakka Identity in China and Abroad. N. Constable, ed. Pp. 1–30. Seattle: University of Washington Press.

Mehrotra, Nidhi, and William L. Parish

2001 Daughters, Parents, and Globalization: The Case of Taiwan. *In* Women's Working Lives in East Asia. Mary Brinton, ed. Pp. 298–322. Stanford: Stanford University Press.

Meisner, Maurice

1963 The Development of Formosan Nationalism. China Quarterly 15:691–706.

Mendel, Douglas

1970 The Politics of Formosan Nationalism. Berkeley: University of California Press.

Meskill, Johanna M.

1970 The Chinese Genealogy as a Research Source. *In* Family and Kinship in Chinese Society. Maurice Freedman, ed. Pp. 139–61. Stanford: Stanford University Press.

1979 A Chinese Pioneer Family: The Lins of Wufeng, 1724–1895. Princeton NJ: Princeton University Press.

Miner, Horace

1939 St. Denis: A French Canadian Parish. Chicago: University of Chicago Press.

Mintz, Sidney M.

1981 Afterword. *In* Ahern and Gates 1981:427–42.

Mirsky, Jonathan

1992 Literature of the Wounded. New York Review of Books, 5 March: 6–10.

Morley, James W.

1993 Driven by Growth: Political Change in the Asia-Pacific Region. Armonk NY: M. E. Sharpe.

Moskowitz, Marc L.

2001 The Haunting Fetus: Abortion, Sexuality, and the Spirit World in Taiwan. Honolulu: University of Hawaii Press.

Mueller, Eva

1977 The Impact of Demographic Factors on Economic Development in Taiwan. Population and Development Review 3:1–23.

Murphy, H. B. M.

1982 Review of Normal and Abnormal Behavior in Chinese Culture by A. Kleinman and T. Y Lin. Transcultural Psychiatric Research 14:37–40.

Murray, Stephen O.

1978 Tu, vous, usted. Papers in Linguistics 11:261–69.

1981 Die ethnoromantische Versuchung. *In* Der Wissenschaftler und das Irrationale. Hans-Peter Duerr, ed. Vol. 1, pp. 377–85. Frankfurt a/M.: Syndikat.

1982 The Dissolution of Classical Ethnoscience. Journal of the History of the Behavioral Sciences 18:163–75.

1983a   The Creation of Linguistic Structure. American Anthropologist 85:356–62.

1983b   Fuzzy Sets and "Abominations." Man 19:396–99.

1986   Nonsensical "Cultural Consensus." Partially published in American Anthropologist 89:443–44.

1988   The Reception of Anthropological Work in American Sociology, 1921–1951. Journal of the History of the Behavioral Sciences 24:135–51.

1991   The Rights of Research Assistants and the Rhetoric of Political Suppression: Morton Grodzins and the University of California Japanese-American Evacuation and Resettlement Study. Journal of the History of the Behavioral Sciences 27:130–56.

1994a   Subordinating Native Cosmologies to the Empire of Gender. Current Anthropology 35:59–61.

1994b   Theory Groups in the Study of Language in North America: A Social History. Amsterdam: John Benjamin.

1999   The Non-Eclipse of Americanist Anthropology during the 1930s and 40s. In The Americanist Tradition in Anthropology. Regna Darnell and Lisa Valentine, eds. Pp. 52–74. Toronto: University of Toronto Press.

2002   Francis L. K. Hsu. In Celebrating a Century of the American Anthropological Association: Presidential Portraits. Regna Darnell, ed. Pp. 245–48. Lincoln: University of Nebraska Press.

2005   American Anthropologists Discover Peasants. In Histories of Anthropology Annual, vol. I. Regna Darnell and Frederic W. Gleach, eds. Pp. 000–000. Lincoln: University of Nebraska Press.

Murray, Stephen O., and Keelung Hong

1988   Taiwan, China, and the "Objectivity" of Dictatorial Elites. American Anthropologist 90:976–78.

1991   American Anthropologists Looking through Taiwanese Culture. Dialectical Anthropology 16:273–99.

1994   Taiwanese Culture, Taiwanese Society. Lanham MD: University Press of America.

Myers, Ramon H., and Adrienne Ching

1964   Agricultural Development in Taiwan under Japanese Colonialism. Journal of Asian Studies 23:550–70.

Needham, Rodney

1985   Exemplars. Berkeley: University of California Press.

Ng Mi-Yen

1988   Zen ni Mahzo (Thousand-Year Mahzo). Daiba: Tzin Gan.

Nickerson, Peter

2001   A Poetics and Politics of Possession: Taiwanese Spirit-Medium Cults and Autonomous Popular Cultural Space. Positions 9:187–217.

Passin, Herbert
    1947    A Note on Japanese Research in Formosa. American Anthropologist 49:514–18.
    1982    Encounter with Japan. Tokyo: Kodansha.
Pan Ying-Hai
    1994    Settlements, History, and Meaning: The Development of Settlements and Ethnic Relations of T'ou-she Village. Bulletin of the Institute of Ethnology, Academia Sinica 77:89–123.
Park, Robert E., and Herbert A. Miller
    1921    Old World Traits Transplanted. New York: Harper.
Pasternak, Burton
    1968    Atrophy of Patrilineal Bonds in a Chinese Village in Historical Perspective. Ethnohistory 15:293–327.
    1972    Kinship and Community in Two Chinese Villages. Stanford: Stanford University Press.
    1983    Sociology and Anthropology in China: Revitalization and Its Constraints. In The Social Sciences and Fieldwork in China: Views from the Field. A. Thurston and B. Pasternak. Pp. 37–62. Boulder CO: Westview.
    1989    Age at First Marriage in a Taiwanese Locality, 1916–1945. Journal of Family History 14:91–117.
Peace, William J.
    2004    Leslie A. White: Evolution and Revolution in Anthropology. Lincoln: University of Nebraska Press.
Phillips, Herbert P.
    1973    Some Premises of American Scholarship on Thailand. In Western Values and Southeast Asian Scholarship. J. Fischer. Pp. 446–66. Berkeley: Center for South and Southeast Asian Studies.
Price, David H.
    1998    Cold War Anthropology: Collaborators and Victims of the National Security State. Identities 4:389–430.
    2002a    Present Dangers, Past Wars, and Past Anthropologies. Anthropology Today 18(1):3–5.
    2002b    Lessons from Second World War Anthropology. Anthropology Today 18(3):14–20.
    2004a    Standing Up for Academic Freedom: The Case of Irving Goldman. Anthropology Today 20(4):16–21.
    2004b    Threatening Anthropology: McCarthyism and the FBI's Surveillance of Activist Anthropologists. Durham NC: Duke University Press.
Redfield, Robert
    1940    The Folk Culture of the Yucatán. Chicago: University of Chicago Press.
    1954    Community Studies in Japan and China. Far Eastern Quarterly 14:3–10.

1955 The Little Community: Viewpoints for the Study of a Human Whole. Chicago: University of Chicago Press.

Redfield, Robert, Ralph Linton, and Melville J. Herskovits

1936 Memorandum for the Study of Acculturation. American Anthropologist 38:149–52.

Reischauer, Edwin O.

1981 The Japanese. Cambridge MA: Harvard University Press.

Riggins, Stephen H.

1997 The Rhetoric of Othering. In The Language and Politics of Exclusion: Others in Discourse. S. Riggins, ed. Pp. 1–30. Thousand Oaks CA: Sage.

Robin, Ron

2001 The Making of the Cold War Enemy. Princeton NJ: Princeton University Press.

Rofel, Lisa

2003 The Outsider Within: Margery Wolf and Feminist Anthropology. American Anthropologist 105:596–604.

Rohsenow, Hill Gates

1973a Review of Gods, Ghosts, and Ancestors: The Folk Religion of a Taiwanese Village by David K. Jordan. Journal of Asian Studies 33:478–80.

1973b Review of Kinship and Community in Two Chinese Villages by Burton Pasternak. Journal of Asian Studies 33:476–78.

1975 Review of Religion in Chinese Society, edited by Arthur P. Wolf. Journal of Asian Studies 35:487–99.

Rosch, Eleanor

1977 Human Categorization. Studies in Cross-Cultural Categorization 1:1–49.

Roth, Julius

1974 Professionalism: The Sociologists' Decoy. Sociology of Work and Occupations 1:6–23.

Rubinstein, Murray A.

1994 The Other Taiwan: 1945 to the Present. Armonk NY: M. E. Sharpe.

Said, Edward

1978 Orientalism. New York: Vintage.

Samarin, William J.

1972 Tongues of Men and Angels: The Religious Language of Pentecostalism. New York: Macmillan.

Sandel, Todd L.

2003 Linguistic Capital in Taiwan: The KMT's Mandarin Language Policy and Its Perceived Impact on Language Practices of Bilingual Mandarin and Tai-gi Speakers. Language in Society 32:523–51.

Sangren, P. Steven

    1987   History and Magical Power in a Chinese Community. Stanford: Stanford University Press.

    2001   Chinese Sociologics: An Anthropological Account of the Role of Alienation in Social Reproduction. London: Athlone.

Schak, David C.

    1991   Assistance to Poor Relatives: Chinese Kinship Reconsidered. Journal of Oriental Studies 27:111–39.

Schatz, Sara

    2000   Elites, Masses, and the Struggle for Democracy in Mexico: A Culturalist Approach. Westport CT: Praeger.

Schneider, David M.

    1968   American Kinship: A Cultural Account. Toronto: Prentice Hall.

Shepherd, John R.

    1993   Statecraft and Political Economy on the Taiwan Frontier, 1600–1800. Stanford: Stanford University Press.

Shweder, Richard A.

    1991   Thinking Through Cultures. Cambridge MA: Harvard University Press.

Simon, Scott

    2000   Entrepreneurship and Empowerment: Experiences of Taiwanese Businesswomen. Anthropology of Work Review 21(3):19–24.

    2003a   Contesting Formosa: Tragic Remembrance, Urban Space, and National Identity in Taipak. Identities 10:109–31.

    2003b   Sweet and Sour: Life Worlds of Taipei Women Entrepreneurs. Lanham MD: Rowman and Littlefield.

Siu, Helen F.

    1993   Cultural Identity and the Politics of Difference in South China. Dædalus 122(2):19–43.

Siu, Paul Chan Pang

    1952   The Sojourner. American Journal of Sociology 58:34–44.

    1987 [1953]   The Chinese Laundryman: A Study of Social Isolation. New York: New York University Press.

Skinner, G. William

    1954   A Study of Chinese Community Leadership in Bangkok Together with an Historical Survey of Chinese Society in Thailand. PhD diss., Cornell University. (Revised version published in 1958 by Cornell University Press.)

    1964   Marketing and Social Structure in Rural China. Journal of Asian Studies 24:3–23.

Smith, Robert J.

    1983   Japanese Society. Cambridge University Press.

1989  Something Old, Something New: Tradition and Culture in the Study of Japan. Journal of Asian Studies 48:715–23.

Smith, Robert J., and John B. Cornell

1956  Two Japanese Villages. Ann Arbor: Center for Japanese Studies.

Sneider, Vern

1951  The Teahouse of the August Moon. New York: Putnam.

1953  A Pail of Oysters. New York: Putnam.

1956  A Long Way from Home, and Other Stories. New York: Putnam.

1960  The King from Ashtabula. New York: Putnam.

Speare, Alden, Jr., Paul Liu, and Ching-Lung Tsay

1988  Urbanization and Development: The Rural-Urban Transition in Taiwan. Boulder CO: Westview.

Spicer, Edward H.

1940  Pascua: A Yaqui Village in Arizona. Chicago: University of Chicago Press.

Spiro, Melford E.

1967  Burmese Supernaturalism. Englewood Cliffs NJ: Prentice-Hall.

1993  Is the Western Conception of the Self "Peculiar" within the Context of World Cultures? Ethos 21:107–53.

Stafford, Charles

1992  Good Sons and Virtuous Mothers: Kinship and Chinese Nationalism in Taiwan. Man 27:363–78.

1995  The Roads of Chinese Childhood: Learning and Identification in Angang. Cambridge: Cambridge University Press.

2000  Separation and Religion in Modern China. Cambridge: Cambridge University Press.

Starn, Orin

1986  Engineering Internment: Anthropologists and the War Relocation Authority. American Ethnologist 13:700–720.

Sternberg, Leo

1927  Divine Election in Primitive Religion. Compte rendu de la XXIe session, Congrès international des Américanistes 2:472–512.

Steward, Julian

1950  Area Research. Social Science Research Council Bulletin 63.

1956  The People of Puerto Rico: A Study in Social Anthropology. Urbana: University of Illinois Press.

Su Bing

1986  Taiwan's 400 Year History. Washington DC: Taiwanese Cultural Grassroots Association.

Sugimoto, Y.

1971  Japanese in Taiwan. Current Trends in Linguistics 8:969–95.

Sutlive, Vinson H., Jr.

1992  The Iban *Manang* in the Sibu District of the Third Division of

Sarawak. *In* Oceanic Homosexualities. Stephen O. Murray, ed. Pp. 273–
84. New York: Garland.

Suzuki, Mitsuo
1976    The Shamanistic Element in Taiwanese Folk Religion. *In* The
Realm of the Extra-Human: Agents and Audiences. Agehananda Bharati,
ed. Pp. 253–60. The Hague: Mouton.

Suzuki, Peter T.
1981    Anthropologists in the Wartime Camps for Japanese Americans.
Dialectical Anthropology 6:23–60.

Suzuki Takao
1978    Japanese and the Japanese: Words in Culture. San Francisco:
Kodansha International.

Tambiah, Stanley J.
1970    Buddhism and the Spirit Cults in Northeast Thailand. Cambridge:
Cambridge University Press.

Tan Chung-Min
1967    Ancestor Worship and Clan Organization in a Rural Village of
Taiwan. Bulletin of the Institute of Ethnology, Academia Sinica 23:192–
224.

Tang Mei Chun
1978    Urban Chinese Families: An Anthropological Field Study in Taipei
City, Taiwan. Taipei: National Taiwan University Press.

Taeuber, Irene B.
1974    Migrants and Cities in Japan, Taiwan, and Northeastern China. *In*
The Chinese City between Two Worlds. Mark Elvin and G. W. Skinner,
eds. Pp. 359–84. Stanford: Stanford University Press.

Thelin, Mark
1977    Two Taiwanese Villages. Daidiong: Dunghai University.

Thomas, W. I., and Florian Znaniecki
1927 [1918–20]    The Polish Peasant in America and Europe. New
York: Knopf.

Thurston, Anne F., and Burton Pasternak
1983    The Social Sciences and Fieldwork in China: Views from the Field.
Boulder CO: Westview.

Trix, Frances
1993    Spiritual Discourse: Learning with an Islamic Master. Philadelphia:
University of Pennsylvania Press.

Tseng Min-Chieh
2001    The Changes of Gender Differences in Earnings in Taiwan: 1982,
1992, and 2000. Journal of Population Studies 23:147–209.

Tseng Wen-Shing
1973    Psychiatric Study of Shamanism in Taiwan. Archives of General
Psychiatry 26:561–65.

Tsuah Siung-Hwei

1989   Daiwan e Ong-Ia ga Mahzo (Ong-Ya and Mahzo of Taiwan). Daiba: Dai Guan.

Tu, Edward J. C., Vicki A. Freedman, and Douglas A. Wolf

1992   Kinship and Family Support in Taiwan. Research on Aging 15:465–86.

Tuchman, Barbara

1971   Stillwell and the American Experience in China, 1911–1945. New York: Macmillan.

Turner, Edith

1992   Experiencing Ritual. Philadelphia: University of Pennsylvania Press.

1999   Experiental Shamanism and Its Implications for the World of Knowledge. Ethnological Studies of Shamanism and Other Indigenous Beliefs and Practices 52:205–22.

Van der Geest, Sjaak

2003   Confidentiality and Pseudonyms. Anthropology Today 19(1):14–18.

Veyne, Paul

1988   Did the Greeks Believe in Their Myths? Chicago: University of Chicago Press.

Vogt, Evan Z., and Ethel M. Albert

1966   People of Rimrock: A Study of Values in Five Cultures. Cambridge MA: Harvard University Press.

Wachman, Alan M.

1994   Taiwan: National Identity and Democratization. Armonk NY: M. E. Sharpe.

Wafer, Jim

1991   The Taste of Blood: Spirit Possession in Brazilian Candomblé. Philadelphia: University of Pennsylvania Press.

Wallace, Anthony F. C.

1952   Individual Differences and Cultural Uniformities. American Sociological Review 17:747–50.

1956   Revitalization Movements. American Anthropologist 58:274–81.

1970   The Death and Rebirth of the Seneca. New York: Knopf.

2003   Revitalization and Mazeways. Lincoln: University of Nebraska Press.

Wallace, Anthony F. C., and John Atkins

1960   The Meaning of Kinship Terms. American Anthropologist 62:58–80.

Wang Fu-Chang

1994   Ethnic Assimilation and Mobilization: An Analysis of Party Support in Taiwan. Bulletin of the Institute of Ethnology, Academia Sinica 77:1–34.

2002a   Toward Theories of Ethnic Relations in Taiwan. Taiwanese Sociology 4:1–10.

2002b   Ethnic Contact or Ethnic Competition? Explaining Regional Differences in Ethnic Consciousness. Taiwanese Sociology 4:11–74.

Wang Horng-Luen

2000   Rethinking the Global and the National: Reflections on National Imaginations in Taiwan. Theory, Culture and Society 17(4):93–117.

Wang Hong-Zen

2001   Ethnicized Social Mobility in Taiwan. Modern China 27:328–58.

2002   Class Structures and Social Mobility in Taiwan in the Initial Post-War Period. China Journal 48:55–85.

Warren, Mark E.

2000   Democracy and Association. Princeton NJ: Princeton University Press.

Watson, James L.

1976   Review of Religion and Ritual in Chinese Society by Arthur Wolf. China Quarterly 66:355–64.

Watson, Rubie S.

1986   The Named and the Nameless: Gender and Person in Chinese Society. American Ethnologist 13:619–31.

Wax, Murray L.

1984   "Religion" as Universal: Tribulations of an Anthropological Enterprise. Zygon 19:5–20.

Weller, Robert P.

1985   Bandits, Beggars, and Ghosts: The Failure of State Control over Religious Interpretations in Taiwan. American Ethnologist 12:46–61.

1986   Alternate Civilities: Democracy and Culture in China and Taiwan. Boulder CO: Westview.

1987a   Unities and Diversities in Chinese Religion. Seattle: University of Washington Press.

1987b   The Politics of Ritual Disguise: Repression and Response in Taiwanese Popular Religion. Modern China 13:17–39.

1994   Resistance, Chaos, and Control in China: Taiping Rebels, Taiwanese Ghosts, and Tiananmen. Seattle: University of Washington Press.

1999   Alternate Civilities: Democracy and Culture in China and Taiwan. Boulder CO: Westview.

2000   Living at the Edge: Religion, Capitalism, and the End of the Nation-State in Taiwan. Public Culture 12:477–98.

Wen, Lily

2000   Colonialism, Gender, and Work: A Voice from the People of the Lily and the Leopard. Anthropology of Work Review 21(3):24–27.

Wikan, Unni

    1980   Life among the Poor in Cairo. London: Tavistock.

    1990   Managing Turbulent Hearts: A Balinese Formula for Living. Chicago: University of Chicago Press.

    1992   Beyond the Words: The Power of Resonance. American Ethnologist 19:460–82.

Wilen, Tracey

    1995   Asia for Women on Business: Hong Kong, Taiwan, Singapore, and South Korea. Berkeley: Stone Bridge Press.

Williams, Jack F.

    1988   Urban and Regional Planning in Taiwan: The Quest for Balanced Regional Development. Tijdschrift voor economische en sociale geografie 79:175–81.

    1989   Paying the Price of Economic Development in Taiwan: Environmental Degradation. Journal of Oriental Studies 27:58–78.

Winckler, Edwin A.

    1994   Cultural Policy on Postwar Taiwan. *In* Harrell and Huang 1994:22–46.

Winckler, Edwin A., and Susan M. Greenhalgh

    1988   Contending Approaches to the Political Economy of Taiwan. Armonk NY: M. E. Sharpe.

Winkelman, Michael J.

    1990   Shamans and Other "Magico-Religious" Healers: A Cross-Cultural Study of Their Origins, Nature, and Social Transformations. Ethos 18:308–52.

Winks, Robin W.

    1987   Cloak and Gown: Scholars in the Secret War: Scholars in the Secret War. New York: Morrow.

Wittfogel, Karl A.

    1957   Oriental Despotism. New Haven: Yale University Press.

Wolf, Arthur P.

    1974   Religion and Ritual in Chinese Society. Stanford: Stanford University Press.

    1981   Domestic Organization. *In* Ahern and Gates 1981:341–60.

    1985   The Study of Chinese Society on Taiwan. *In* Hsieh and Chuang 1985:3–26.

    1995   Sexual Attraction and Childhood Association: A Chinese Brief for Edward Westermarck. Stanford: Stanford University Press.

Wolf Arthur P., and Chieh-Shang Huang

    1980   Marriage and Adoption in China. Stanford: Stanford University Press.

Wolf, Eric R.

    1966   Peasants. Toronto: Prentice Hall.

1969    Peasant Wars of the Twentieth Century. New York: Harper and Row.

Wolf, Margery

1968    The House of Lim. London: Prentice Hall.

1972    Women and the Family in Rural Taiwan. Stanford: Stanford University Press.

1990    The Woman Who Didn't Become a Shaman. American Ethnologist 17:419–30.

1992    A Thrice Told Tale: Feminism, Postmodernism, and Ethnographic Responsibility. Stanford: Stanford University Press.

Wong, Timothy Ka-ing

2001    From Ethnic to Civic Nationalism: The Formation and Changing Nature of Taiwanese Identity. Asian Perspective 25:175–206.

Woolard, Kathryn A.

1985    Language Variation and Cultural Hegemony. American Ethnologist 12:738–48.

1988    Double Talk: The Politics of Ethnicity in Catalonia. Stanford: Stanford University Press.

Wright, Arthur F.

1953    Studies in Chinese Thought. American Anthropological Association Memoir 7. Chicago: University of Chicago Press.

Wu, David Yen-Ho

1990    Chinese Minority Policy and the Meaning of Minority Culture: The Example of the Bai in Yunnan, China. Human Organization 49:1–13.

1997    McDonald's in Taipei: Hamburgers, Betel Nuts, and National Identity. *In* Golden Arches East: McDonald's in East Asia. James L. Watson, ed. Pp. 110–35. Stanford: Stanford University Press.

Wu Nai-Teh

1992    Party Support and National Identities: Social Cleavages and Party Competition in Taiwan. Bulletin of the Institute of Ethnology, Academia Sinica 74:33–61.

2002    Identity Conflict and Political Trust: Ethnic Politics in Contemporary Taiwan. Taiwanese Sociology 4:75–118.

Xu Xiaohe and Lai Shu-Chuan

2002    Resources, Gender Ideologies, and Marital Power: The Case of Taiwan. Journal of Family Issues 23:209–45.

Yager, Joseph A.

1988    Transforming Agriculture in Taiwan: The Experience of the Joint Commission on Rural Reconstruction. Ithaca NY: Cornell University Press.

Yang, Martin M. C.

1945    A Chinese Village: Taitou, Shangtung Province. New York: Columbia University Press.

1970    Socio-Economic Results of Land Reform in Taiwan. Honolulu: East-West Center Press.

Yang, Mayfair Mei-hui

2002    The Resilience of Guanxi and Its New Deployments. China Quarterly 170:459–76.

Yi Chin-Chun and Chien Wen-Yin

2001    The Continual Employment Patterns of Married Women in Taiwan: A Compromise between Family and Work. Taiwanese Sociology 1:149–82.

You Ying-Lung

1994    Party Image, Ideology, and Secular Realignment in Taiwan. Bulletin of the Institute of Ethnology, Academia Sinica 78:61–99.

Young, Virginia Heyer

2005    Ruth Benedict: Beyond Relativity, Beyond Pattern. Lincoln: University of Nebraska Press.

Yu Guang-Hong

1986    No Property, No Ancestral Tablet? A Reanalysis of Emily Ahern's Chinan Data. Bulletin of the Institute of Ethnology, Academica Sinica 62:115–77.

Yu Shuenn-Der

1996    Opposition and Compromise: An Analysis of the Relationship between Night Market Traders and Taiwan's State. Bulletin of the Institute of Ethnology, Academia Sinica 82:115–74.

Yu Wei-Hsin

2001    Taking Informality into Account: Women's Work in the Formal and Informal Sectors in Taiwan. In Women's Working Lives in East Asia. Mary Brinton, ed. Pp. 233–62. Stanford: Stanford University Press.

# Index

"client" (*ke-ren*), 90–91, 120–21
Cohen, Myron, 54, 56, 58
Cold War, 17–18, 22, 40
Cole, Fay Cooper, 14
colonialism, general, 6–7. *See also* Japanese (colonial) empire; Q'ing (Manchu) dynasty
Columbia University, 66, 67
community studies, 16–17, 18, 52–54, 55–56, 62
Confucianism, 31, 59, 73, 82, 92, 102, 103
corruption, 33–34, 39
Cultural Revolution, Great Proletarian, 28, 109

Daiba (Taipei), 67, 121n31
Dailam (Tainan), 65
*dang-gí*, 69, 77–97, 112–13, 121n29, 122–27
Daoism, 50, 82
deference, 100–101
DeGlopper, Donald, 51, 69
Democratic Progressive Party (DPP), 22, 37, 106
democratization, 6, 7–8, 30, 104, 106–9
dependency theory, 73
Diamond, Norma, 65, 66, 71, 72
divination, 122n7
division of household (*pun ke-hoe*), 49
divorce, 79–80, 122n6
Durkheim, Émile, 55, 118n5, 127n31
Dutch East Indies Company, vii, 19, 60

Eberhard, Wolfram, 64
education, 3–4, 7–8, 20–21, 109
embourgeoisement, 87
endogamy, 122n5
entrepreneurs, 46, 116n3
environmental movement, 107–8, 121n31
ethnography, 57–58, 65–66, 71–73, 109.
    *See also* community studies
ethnomedicine, 68–71, 120–21
ethnosemantics, 55, 70, 96, 108, 121n27, 28, 127n31
Ewing, Katherine, 83–84, 94, 102, 126n25, 126n29

family (*ge*), 49–54, 55, 67, 78–82, 91,

98–103; bilateral, 99, 108; joint, 52; uterine, 102, 124–25
farmer movement (1980s), 47, 123n13
Farquhar, Judith, 121n29
Fei, John, 45
"feminist," 124n19
Foster, George, 16
freedom of the press, 23, 32–33, 58
Freeman, Derek, 112–13
Fried, Morton, 57–58, 61, 62
Fujian, 19, 20

Gallin, Bernard, 18, 43–46, 48, 53, 54, 56, 58, 65, 66, 69, 118n2, 120n24
Gallin, Rita, 48, 53, 58, 71–72, 80, 81, 120n24
Gates, Hill, 5, 6, 45, 51, 55, 58, 59, 60, 63, 68, 71, 73, 105, 106, 119n15
Gellner, Ernest, 8
gender, as explanatory variable, 83, 86, 94–97, 101, 108, 123n14, 125n24
geomancy (*hong-sui*), 68
ghosts, 95, 127n30
Giles, Linda, 86
Gold, Thomas, 6, 10, 22
Gou Eng-Chu, 41
Gower, Charlotte, 16
Guan Gong, 123n7

Hakka, 11, 32, 50, 60, 104, 127n3, 128n1
Harrell, Stevan, 22, 106, 115n4
Harvard University Russian Research Center, 17
Hinduism, 89, 118n4
Ho, Samuel, 44, 45, 46
Holbrook, Bruce, 120–21
Holo (/Hokkien), 3, 11, 32, 50, 60, 78, 80, 83, 100, 104, 122n7, 124nn16–17, 125n23, 128n1
Hong Keelung, viii, 3–5, 51, 71, 91, 95–98, 77, 113–14
Hong Kong, 92, 100, 103, 113, 123n10, 127n1
Hoover Institution, 5, 27–38, 41, 117n3, 4
household registries, 35, 49, 51–54, 62, 64, 118nn6–8
Hsu, Francis, 17, 65, 120n22

**In the Critical Studies in the
History of Anthropology series**

Milton Keynes UK
Ingram Content Group UK Ltd.
UKHW010942050324
438675UK00012B/448